MAKING THE
Supernatural
Normal.

TAKING GOD'S POWER OUTSIDE THE DOORS OF YOUR CHURCH

JARED STEPP

SUPERNATURAL TRUTH PRODUCTIONS, LLC
Practical Training for Spirit-Filled Living
www.SupernaturalTruth.com

Making the Supernatural Normal:
Mobilizing the Local Church to Take God's Power Outside Its Doors
By Jared Stepp

© Copyright 2023, Jared Stepp.

ISBN: 978-1-959547-00-6

Table of Contents

Section 1:
The Supernatural is Personal

(My story)

Chapter 1 –

Ruined in the Best Way

Falling asleep underneath a pew is a unique skill, only accessible to highly trained 8-year-olds. I had mastered it—the cushionless feel of carpet-on-concrete under the shoulder blades, turning your head so you don't breathe in too many fuzzies from under the seat (but not so much that you wake up with a Berber-carpet-patterned rugburn on your cheek). Don't get up too fast; it leads to headaches. Check for drool. Then stay drowsy long enough that hopefully someone carries you to the car.

It was a dance really.

I loved every second of these 24-hour prayer meetings. While other kids went to sleep to the flashing of a TV in their room (not in my house!), or their parents fighting, or to the Super Mario Bros. theme song on repeat, I went to sleep with a whole chorus of other noises in the ambiance: The sound of a band playing Jewish-style, fast worship songs or slow, flowing songs with the unique sound of bells-piano on the keyboard. I fell asleep to the sound of people screaming out to God for His presence to fall in the room, for revival in our nation, for the lost peoples of the world to be called in to Jesus from the north, south, east, and west.

Every once in a while, I'd start falling asleep on a Sunday night only to hear the strange sounds of an exorcism. Oh, I'd get up for that! You couldn't sleep on that one. Regularly, I'd hear prophetic words given with pinpoint accuracy, tongues that were interpreted, and set people free. Out of the corner of my eye slits, I'd see people get prayed for who would fall or shake or get flushed in the face. These same people would report physical healings later, deliverance from 15 years of nicotine addiction in a moment, and other, even greater claims like salvation, sin being taken away, or having a vision of Jesus. But certainly, *I was ruined for a normal prayer meeting.* I was ruined for church with two choruses and a hymn—for stand up, sit down, take the elements, try not to die of boredom "church." I was ruined for three-points-and-a-poem sermons. When my dad or the missionaries, evangelists, and others stepped to the pulpit, they had a WORD FROM GOD, and they would CALL THE FIRE OF THE HOLY SPIRIT DOWN!

But I'm not sure any of that would have been completely enough without a couple breakthrough moments in my life.

BREAKTHROUGH 1 . . .

I sat on the white speckled linoleum of a fluorescent-lit hallway, contemplating if I wanted to act like an alligator to attack the other kids' ankles or a jaguar, when out of the room popped 9-year-old Kevin. Kevin was decked out, head to toe, in a Royal Ranger (Christian scouts) dress khaki uniform with more badges than a Brigadier General on his chest. So, obviously, when he spoke, I listened. He announced in the hallway that we were going to pray for my 8-year-old brother Shawn's leg. So, I jumped to attention and ran over to the group of 5 or 6 boys who sat down with Shawn's leg stretched out on the floor. We all prayed—fast and passionate (we didn't have 24-hour attention spans!). Kevin led. I watched as my brother's leg grew, and all the boys agreed that it happened. We jumped up to tell anyone we could find what we saw God do. And the most amazing thing happened: no one poured water on our enthusiasm. They just listened, saw Shawn walk without a hitch for the first time in his life, and praised God with us!

I watched my brother over the next few years develop into a star athlete who could dunk a basketball at 5'7". He was so good that sometimes I wondered if God had healed him a little *too* much that night. You know—a little super-powered.

None of that was possible before those boys prayed that night. No one had convinced us of what God couldn't do. We read the Bible, knew the Bible, and believed the Bible. Therefore, we saw Jesus do a Bible-level miracle. It was quite simple. Watching your brother's leg grow in front of your face as a 5-year-old—that'll mess you up in the best way.

BREAKTHROUGH 2 . . .

Laying on the floor, eyes closed, incapable of movement—my 12-year-old brain processed a symphony of noises all around the room: loud praying, yelling, and singing, "More, Lord!" repeatedly (the same prayer that sent me to the floor without anyone touching me). But there were also weird noises: someone roaring like a lion in one corner, someone else acting like they're giving birth behind me, someone barking like a dog in the other corner, and laughter—not like "someone told a good joke" laughter but rather embarrassing, uncontrollable, loud and awkward laughter. Those sounds were generally accompanied by abnormal movement—shaking, jerking, doubling over, or convulsing like a person being electrocuted. All of that would have freaked me right out and caused me to scream, "Fakers!" except for the undeniable work that God was doing in me.

As I lay paralyzed, God began to speak to me and confirm in specific and unavoidable ways many things He'd been telling me about my future and ministry. On the screen of my imagination, He flashed vision after vision of things He had for me and that I would do for Him. Those things all happened. His words all came true. Twenty-five years later, I still remember many of those words, visions, and fulfillments.

If you want to call it emotionalism or excessive, you're entitled to that opinion. You'd be wrong though. Were there people who embellished a little? Maybe. But when God shows up undeniably in your life, you might freak out too. There have been excesses in every gathering of believers from the beginning, but in a move of God, we put our excesses out in the open so we can grow from them and learn (rather than all the private sin of other believers).

Also, in a move of God, those excesses are the exceptions that prove the authentic work of God in people's lives. I know God was moving, and He was aggressively and consistently pushing me out of my comfort zone.

Throughout Jesus's life, He aggressively and consistently pushed people out of their comfort zones. As you study the Gospels, this is one thread that doesn't go away. Jesus was a pusher. Jesus militantly crushed barriers within which people were personally and spiritually comfortable. He only and always broke down the barriers that would separate people from God. Personal space? Crushed. Self-righteousness? Crushed. Earthly thinking? Crushed. Doubt in His power and goodness? Crushed. Every time. He aggressively pushed people into a place of encounter with God.

Jesus is still aggressively pushing people out of their comfort zones and into authentic encounters with His Father. Ask Him right now: In what ways am I too comfortable? When I come to church, what are my next steps toward encounter with You? In my prayer time right now, Holy Spirit, please invade my comfort zone and bring me into Your growth.

BREAKTHROUGH 3 . . .

Gunshots every night. This was not the generally advisable environment in which to keep 40+ teenagers. Yet there we were, in San Quintin, Mexico, on the Baja California Peninsula, sleeping in little places beside migrant worker camps that were barely livable.

Thank God, I had youth pastors who were willing to take us toward the danger rather than away! Each day, we would split into four groups, divvy up food (like a yummy oatmeal), and drive to different migrant worker camps to feed about one hundred hungry kids.

My group pulled up to a large, ominous, fenced-in area that day. No one was in sight. We thought it was a dud. But no sooner had the gate been opened for us than kids started pouring out of shanty houses. It seemed like they were spawning out of the desert sand itself. There was a sea of kids there.

We only had one hundred servings of food.

Their parents were the ones shooting and revolting the night before.

This was not good.

Even as a 14-year-old, I knew what to do. We prayed, "God, you see these kids. Multiply this food so they can be blessed ... *and* so we don't die."

Then a 15-year-old girl and I (who I might or might not have had a crush on) began to scoop out the food into the cups. We both felt in our hearts and agreed to give out the same amount of food we would have for only one hundred kids. We gave generous servings. And we went through seven hundred cups that day.

Every child ate and was satisfied, and we even had food left over. The exhilaration of that moment obscured my hand cramps as we powered through. That girl and I *knew* what God had done. Everyone there was witness to it. God loved those kids so much that He wanted to bless them. He loved us so much that He wanted us to not die. And He loved His reputation so much that He wanted these kids to have a good first experience with Christians.

There are many other moments I've experienced with God, but these were some that ruined me and threw undeniable authenticity on other times Jesus chose to show up and show off in my life.

_____

Discuss/Reflect

1. What were some of your earliest encounters with God? How did faith begin to rise in your heart? Have you been able to glean faith from other people's stories as well as your own?
2. How are you too comfortable in your life with God?
3. When you come to church, what are your next steps toward encounter with God? In prayer right now say, "Holy Spirit, please invade my comfort zone and bring me into Your growth!"

STUDY

Read John 1:43-51 (Jesus calls Philip and Nathanael). Ask Jesus to speak to you as you read.

What stood out to you about Jesus's call to Nathanael? What stirred in your spirit as you read?

_____

_____

_____

Nathanael was completely "all-in" with Jesus after a simple word of knowledge. Would that have done it for you? How did Jesus speak Nathanael's heart-language so well?

_____

_____

_____

What are some of the other "greater things" that Jesus would show Nathanael later?

_____

_____

_____

EXERCISE

Ask God to speak your language right now. Ask Him to give you an encounter that will ruin you for ever doing life or church without His presence.

Write down what God says, does or shows you in this moment.

_____

_____

_____

_____

_____

_____

_____

_____

_____

_____

_____

_____

_____

_____

_____

_____

_____

_____

_____

_____

_____

_____

Chapter 2 –
Born of Desperation

"It's a boy!"

Immediately, visions of epic wrestling matches, throwing a football, and playing games together were dancing through my head. Jessica and I were very excited at that sixteen-week checkup.

Then, at twenty weeks, they saw something—maybe a cleft lip on one side, but they weren't sure. We needed to have weekly checkups. Each week, for the next twelve weeks, our news grew worse and worse. The progression was heart-wrenching—from "possibly a cleft lip" to "definitely a cleft, maybe a cleft on both sides" to "definitely a cleft on both sides, maybe a cleft palette" to "definitely a cleft palette, maybe on both sides" to "definitely cleft lip and palette on both sides, and maybe he's got something wrong by his stomach" to "there's a full blockage right above his stomach (in the duodenum), so he can't process food" to my wife's amniotic fluid measuring seven to eight weeks beyond where it should (because he wasn't processing food) to "he, at the very least, has Down-Syndrome and probably has Trisomy 13 or 18" (a death sentence).

Every week, as we went to the appointment, we began to expect this kind of news. We would go home, call our closest family, and cry and pray. I recall frequent prayer meetings in our tiny living room with our close family packed in. We would cry out to God—passionately, fervently, desperately. We had no choice. The medical field had no remedy for us. They recommended an abortion (while he only had a cleft lip), which was horrifying, wrong, and selfish—such a traumatizing proposition for us. That our society would even think of such gratuitous murder when we had a living being, created in the image of God we were fighting for, is, to this day, a source of intense heartbreak and sadness.

We cried out to God again and again. Our prayers were so focused on his cleft lip that we didn't even know fully what we were sowing into. Only months after did God reveal this truth: No prayer is ever wasted.

But I'm ahead of myself. The biggest battles were yet to come.

At 33.5 weeks, my wife was measuring 43 weeks because of all the extra fluid. We had to do a procedure where fluid was removed from her. The risk of doing the procedure was that she would give birth early. The risk of not doing the procedure was the same. We had simply reached the tipping point. As they removed 3.5 liters of fluid from my wife, we gave permission for them to test the fluid (it was out anyway). Then the worst happened: my wife went into labor. They took us from the procedure room to a posh delivery room as Jessica's contractions grew faster and more intense. We had been here before (Jaren was our second). We knew Jessica was giving birth.

The doctor and nurse brought in a stack of papers (medical releases) for us to sign and declared to us the results of their amniotic fluid test: "Your son's lungs are 99% underdeveloped. When he is born, he will not survive the procedures. He will not be able to eat. Your son will die."

Then they left.

Jessica and I remained silent for a minute as I started to sign the papers. Then I stopped and began to pace the room (not the proper move in front of a woman in labor). As I paced, my mind flashed to prayer meeting after prayer meeting, to tears that were cried, to passionate cries to God for hours and hours from the preceding months. Even as I write, tears stream down my face, recalling those precious times where the presence of God graced, empowered, and comforted.

But as I paced the room, there were no tears. There was only anger—*holy* anger. After a couple minutes of praying in the Spirit and recalling the prayers of God's people, what I can only describe as a gift of faith was birthed in me—a holy and unshakeable boldness and tenacity, confidence in God that those prayers weren't wasted. In moment of brash audacity, I shouted, "NO! IT'S NOT GOING DOWN LIKE THIS! They are going to give you food so you can fight this labor, and we are going to walk out of this with their blessing! I'm not signing one more paper!"

Then an amazing miracle happened. My wife, in full out labor, said, "OK!"

We told the medical staff we weren't signing the papers, they need to bring Jessica something to eat, and her labor is going to stop.

The labor stopped. We walked out of the hospital with my wife partially dilated, and the doctor who told us to get the abortion had to sign off on God's miracle.

For the next 6 weeks our prayer meetings continued, but with a different flavor. We had confidence in God, declaring that our son would stay in until he was developed, and he would live.

Finally, my wife was measuring 46 weeks (she was only 39.5 weeks), and it was time. She went into labor, and we were ready and happy, praising God!

We thought we were in the clear, but we weren't. After her water broke, the womb collapsed on Jaren (because it had been so stretched out). I could see his little fingers through my wife's skin. The machines all flatlined—heart rate, oxygen, etc. The scene that followed was what I imagined could only happen on dramatic TV shows, but it is no exaggeration to say that the nurse went running out of the room, screaming down the hallway for the doctor.

Within a couple minutes Jessica was rushed into the operating room. I was left in a dimly lit hallway outside the O.R.

The last sounds I heard were the flatline tones of the machines still monitoring my son.

The first 25 minutes in the hallway, I prayed and remembered all the prayer meetings, the tears, the crying out, and the miracle that had already happened. But here we were again. *Could we experience such an amazing miracle, only to have it ripped away now?*

Then I heard it in my spirit (not with my ears)—the sound of a baby crying. It was beautiful, and it rang in my ears on repeat for the next 20 minutes as I sat praying in the Spirit, in supernatural peace, praising God.

At the 45-minute mark, I heard the same exact sound with my ears from deep inside the large operating room—the sound of my son, ALIVE! God's prophetic sound had become a reality!

This kicked off in my spirit a new hunger for hearing the audio of miracles—the audio of the Spirit.

The whirlwind was just beginning for us. Jaren was brought ought to me in a giant yellow bubble-shield, and I was only allowed to touch his toes. He did have bilateral cleft lip and palette and a duodenal atresia (full blockage in his intestine). He was taken by ambulance to Children's Hospital of Pittsburgh to be prepped for surgery on his stomach so he could eat.

The whirlwind was just beginning. What we had been focused on in prayer hadn't happened the way we prayed, but it seemed like God had siphoned all that prayer and faith toward the moments where our son needed them to live.

No prayer is wasted, even when the object of your prayer expires, when time runs out, when hope seems lost—our God is not capable of wasting prayers. The faith of those moments just got diverted into another place and produced a greater end.

You may be reading, having experienced excruciating and personal loss, having seen prayers that you were passionate about and invested fully in go unanswered. But God is declaring to you: "NO PRAYER IS WASTED!" Let that truth ring in your spirit. Let it mount up in you again and take wings of faith in your heart.

The passion, the investment, the faith of bringing those things to the Lord may not have produced your desired result in the moment, but what if there's another moment coming? What if there's another battle to be fought? And what if God's eyes, looking at your precious prayers and faith, are just beaming with excitement to reveal to you the next answer to the buildup of passion and faith in you?

In hindsight, this started the fire—or at least rekindled and fanned faith into a raging flame in me. It was the fire to see the authentic, supernatural power of God in my life.

I started praying for everyone... *anyone*—every snotty-nosed kid, every bruise, and even mere "allergies." We prayed for them all. Over the next 18 months, I prayed for more than 350 kids and adults with colds, coughs, snotty noses, pneumonia. And I had ZERO PEOPLE GET HEALED!

Zero, besides myself and my immediate family.

Why are you saying this, Pastor? Aren't you trying to build faith?

Yes, wait for it.

I couldn't turn the channel, though. I was compelled to pray for everyone I saw. There was a building of faith in me—a drive and passion that wouldn't be denied. I knew Jesus could. I knew He wanted to. I wasn't going to let my lack of results deter me from His purposes on the earth. So I kept praying.

I can remember vividly the first kid who got healed of croup (barking cough), but that's a story for later. All those prayers, all of that buildup, then, *suddenly*... God started showing up and showing off. "Suddenly" is a funny word when it shows up in the Bible and in your experience. God's sudden move rarely shortcuts the process or the buildup of faith.

Miracles and healings started breaking out in our church, like someone turned on a faucet. It was to the point that in a 3-year period in our church, we saw and recorded more than 300 individual healing stories! These were people who were prayed for individually and then were able to confirm over time that they were completely whole—that the healing that happened in a moment at church was still there over time. It was a healing revival! I had never been a part of anything like it, and honestly, it hasn't stopped to this day. (We'll discuss how to continue in faith in a later chapter.)

This revival demonstrated to me that when people see the authentic power of God, they will not want the weird anymore. Spirit-filled Christians do weird things, thinking it's spiritual, and it turns people off. So you've seen excesses, you've had incorrect prophetic words, you've gotten pushed over at the altar, you've heard people "pray in the spirit" (but you know it's not the Holy Spirit), etc. So have I. The anecdote to inauthentic power, is not *no* power; it's authentic power.

Begin to pray like Jesus and the first Christians. Hunger for the authentic move of God. Invest in it in your secret place, and don't turn the channel until God shows up. Just because our experience to this point doesn't line up with Scripture doesn't mean we should dumb down Scripture to our experience. Instead, we should hold Jesus and the Scripture up as the ideal and not be satisfied until we're living how He taught that we could! If my experience doesn't line up with the Bible, it's my experience that needs to change, not the Bible.

IMPARTATION VERSUS PERSONAL HISTORY

Since that time, I've had people ask me to pray for them for a healing anointing many times, which I am glad to do. Since Jesus is Healer and the Holy Spirit remembers how to do it, He will pour Himself out on anyone who asks. Therefore, if the laying on of my hands can impart anything, I am open.

But there is one item that I cannot impart through the laying on of hands: my personal history with God. What you've seen demonstrated in these chapters is part of my personal history with God. I pray that as you're reading it, faith to see similar breakthroughs raises up in your heart and you begin to believe

God for more. But I cannot pray for you and impart my personal history with God.

Here's the good news: You have your own personal history with God. A history that is earned—that when you remember it, your eyes fill up with tears, your spirit fills up with faith, and your prayers become inspired again.

I cannot impart my personal history with God, but that's the fun part; you get to earn your own. Then the sights, the sounds, the prayers, the moments where you knew beyond any doubt that God showed up and showed off in your life, will sit underneath your prayers as a symphony of faith that crescendos into every supernatural adventure God has for you.

DISCUSS/REFLECT

What are some pieces of your personal history with God that were moments of desperation? Even in those situations where you didn't get what you prayed for, remember the prayers that were prayed. Let them build in your spirit again. No prayer is wasted.

_____

_____

_____

_____

_____

_____

What would it take to get you fired up and start praying for everyone you met?

_____

_____

_____

_____

_____

STUDY

Read Mark 5:24–34 (Woman subject to bleeding). Ask Jesus to speak to you as you read.

What kind of desperation did it take for this woman to pull on Jesus?

_____

_____

_____

Do you think she had prayed to God for healing before?

_____

_____

In verse 32, why did Jesus keep searching after the disciples questioned him?

_____

_____

_____

_____

EXERCISE

Pray something impossible right now (if God doesn't show up, it doesn't happen).

Now, remember the prayers that you've prayed before—the crying out, the prayer meetings, the intensity—no matter what wonderful or misguided thing they were for. Let faith rise up in your heart. Now, pray again for that impossible thing.

Did that feel different?

Pray, "Holy Spirit, light the fire in me to see Your authentic works in everyone I meet."

Now pray it again. (Rinse, repeat.)

Chapter 3 –
God Likes to Talk

What happened next was remarkable. God began to show off more and more in my life, my family, and my church. Miracles, healings, fully confirmed words from Him were regular. It was like the floodgates of heaven were opened.

Now, I had heard God's voice before. At some great moments in my life, I had visions and dreams that I thought were from Him. But those moments were more rare than regular. However, as undeniable confirmations started rolling in, so did the assurance that I was hearing from God.

I began to realize that God likes to talk. As the Good Shepherd (John 10), Jesus is communicating almost all the time. I started to realize the different ways that He communicates.

Also, in praying for an increasingly greater volume of people, I needed God's specific supernatural direction more than ever. Therefore, daily, I was asking Him what He wanted to do, how He wanted to do it, and what was my role in it for specific people in my life. God continued to speak to me through His still, small voice in my spirit, like He had for many years; but He began to also give me many more prophetic pictures.

Pictures and words are the 1-2 punch of God's communication in Scripture. Just as often as a prophet will declare what God said, He will also describe what God showed Him in a picture. While all Scripture is prophetic, roughly one-third of the Bible is written as prophecy. God did that so that we would have a roadmap for hearing from Him more effectively. But many Christians ask God for an answer, listen for the voice in their spirit, never tune in to a picture or anything else, and then leave the place of prayer, thinking they're in a dry spot.

Sometimes God wants to communicate to you more through pictures. Don't worry, He'll still continue speaking too. You'll just hear from Him more when you allow Him to communicate visually also. Pay attention to the pictures you see in prayer.

BACK HEALING VS. NASTYGRAM . . .

Can someone block themselves from the presence of God? Is it possible for the same presence of God that is working on one person to completely miss the person directly next to them? I never knew these were questions I needed to ask, but that's what happens when you enroll in Holy Spirit's school of hearing God's voice. He will give you answers to questions you didn't know you should be asking.

I was sitting in front of a "nastygram" (sort of like a telegram, but less enjoyable to receive). This time, it was in the form of an email from a church member that stated that they didn't like the church, they thought we were making terrible decisions, and particularly they felt that the glory of God had left our church services. That last one especially bothered me.

Rewind 24 hours. I had been asked as the Kid's Pastor to come up from the basement and lead communion for the Sunday morning adult gathering. My dad (my Lead Pastor) decided from time to time to let me loose from my cage and minister to adults too. So, I ministered healing communion—you know: *"He took our infirmities and carried our diseases … by His wounds we are healed … if you need healing in your body, receive it right now as you take the bread and juice …"* That kind of communion.

God was moving in the large auditorium quietly but substantively. It was wonderful. For some reason (in hindsight, it was Holy Spirit), my eye was drawn to a particular row. I saw a friend of mine—a young mom sitting by herself—and I saw God working on her. Then I noticed, a few feet away on the pew, an older man—long time member of the church—sitting as well. They didn't know each other. They just happened to be sitting in the same space.

After the gathering, my friend came bounding up to me, "God healed my lower back. I've had 15 years of intense back pain, and it's completely gone!" We celebrated God's goodness together.

Fast forward again to sitting at my desk the next day, in front of the nastygram, and Holy Spirit dropped in my memory the picture of where my friend and this older man were sitting. He was the one writing the nastygram!

Naturally, anger was my first reaction. I'd like to say it was holy anger, but I'm not so sure that I could blame *that* on God.

Later, I went to Holy Spirit with it to establish what He was teaching me. What did I know? First, God was obviously, undeniably, and verifiably at work in our church services. And second, this man was sitting beside a move of God and did not even recognize it.

I began to think of all the people who heard the Son of God and rejected Him—the many who saw remarkable miracles and grumbled about Him doing them on the Sabbath, who saw the Son of God in the flesh and still were able to shout "Crucify!"

Holy Spirit egged me on, and I asked God questions. *Can someone block themselves from the presence of God? Is it possible for the same presence of God that is working on one person to completely miss the person directly next to them?*

Boom: peace in my spirit. Besides calming my insecurities (which were substantial), Holy Spirit in one moment taught me a timeless principle through four different means: (1) directing circumstances, (2) bringing healing, (3) directing my eyes (He showed me what I needed to see), and (4) supernatural peace when I realized His lesson.

Notice that none of the ways God communicated was with words, or even supernatural vision. That's because God can communicate any way He wants to. In fact, there are at least 27 different ways that God communicates in Scripture (see Appendix B for a list) and enough weird one-offs (hello, donkey!) that it's obvious God can communicate however He wants.

Now, what was the lesson He taught me? People can cut themselves off from the presence of God that's at work in a place through rebellious or sinful attitudes. Just because Holy Spirit is in a room working doesn't mean you're receiving from Him. As believers, we have responsibility to tune in to what He's doing, receive everything He's giving that day, and steward well what He gives.

My friend did that. She tuned in to what God was doing, received Him, and stewarded the testimony well. She was able to share it with many people, and we declared it in front of the church. Testimony is ground for other people to stand on to receive their own breakthroughs. It's very selfish not to share your testimony. And the stewarding of testimony also clears the way for God to do more in your own life. You have a Living Spring, not a broken cistern (Jer. 2:13). You have to give that Living Water away constantly or it becomes stagnant, or even leaks like the cistern.

So, God likes to talk. Are you tuning in to all the different ways?

DISCUSS/REFLECT

What are ways of hearing God's voice you've experienced before? [refer to Appendix B]

_____

_____

_____

_____

What way of hearing God's voice do you need to grow in next? [Appendix B again]

_____

_____

Have you ever felt blocked off from hearing God's voice? Could it have been because of sin or rebellion? How did you tune back in?

_____

_____

_____

_____

_____

_____

_____

_____

_____

STUDY

Read Zechariah 3:1-10. Ask Jesus to speak to you as you read.

How many different ways does God communicate in these verses? List them here.

_____

_____

_____

_____

_____

_____

What are spiritual takeaways you see from each of the communication types?

_____

_____

_____

_____

_____

_____

_____

_____

_____

_____

_____

EXERCISE

Take one minute - Ask God to communicate in a new way to you right now. Write about your experience.

_____

_____

_____

_____

_____

_____

_____

_____

_____

_____

Now pray, "God, I thank you for all the amazing ways You like to communicate. I repent of any attitudes or actions that have kept me from hearing You. Remove any obstacles, in Jesus' name."

Chapter 4 –
What If We Liked to Listen?

During this season, hearing God's voice moved from an obligation to a hobby, a pastime, a joy. It was fun! Every Sunday morning, in the middle of my routine of getting ready for a busy day, I would stop to pray; but it mainly became a time to listen. I began to listen for God's voice, look for His pictures, and receive His marching orders. Asking, "God, what attitude do you want me to approach this day with? What do you want to heal today? What do you want to say today? How can I be a part of your plan?" Then I'd listen.

God likes to talk. What if we like to listen?

I got up from the place of prayer one morning with peace but no specific direction. As I grabbed my office door handle to leave, God said, "You're going to pray for eyes." Cool, let's do this. I had my marching orders. I went downstairs. I could count on one hand the number of eyes I had prayed for in the past year. But that day, before the first gathering even started, four people asked me for prayer for eye healing. To each of them I said, "Come to kids church. God already told me we're praying for eyes." By the end of the day, we had prayed for 8 people for eye healings, and 5 of them were instantly healed.

God likes to talk. What if we liked to listen? The point is that there is no substitute for dedicated time of listening for God's voice. Give Holy Spirit time to teach you—time that is only His.

OUT IN PUBLIC . . .

Eating out became much more fun. I began to ask Holy Spirit to show off when I went out. So, He showed me that in asking Him to show off, I gave up my right to complain about my food and only tip 15%; but it'd be way more exciting! What a trade off! Holy Spirit's school is amazing, profound, and practical.

Dinner with Holy Spirit looked like this: I'd intentionally learn the waiter or waitress's name. (They give you their name at the beginning, so you might as well use it!) Using someone's name is like music to their ears, and it's rare. You'll immediately be seen as personal and kind. Then I'd look for ways to connect with the server. My wife and kids would jump in on this too. "How's your week been?" "How do you remember all of that?" "It's amazing how you can balance all of those!" That inevitably morphs into some kind of conversation. At each moment, I'm asking, "Holy Spirit, what do You have for them? What's Your heart for them?

What's a breakthrough that they need right now? What's a need you want to meet?"

One night, our waitress had a wrist brace on. So, after connecting with her, I simply said, "Hey, can I pray for your wrist?" She started to tear up (people are shocked in a good way by genuine kindness).

"Yes … for sure."

We prayed for her. No fireworks. She didn't take the brace off and start running and shouting. Nope. But the sweet and powerful presence of God was ministering to her. As I prayed, I kept being drawn to her right shoulder, so then I asked, "Do you have something going on with your right shoulder too?"

"Yes," she answered hesitantly (implying, "How did you know?").

I said, "God showed me that you have pain there, and He only does that if He wants to heal it. Can I pray for that too?"

"Yes."

So, we prayed again. Again, no fireworks.

She simply said, "Thank you so much." And that was it. I don't even know if she was healed. But that's not even the point. The point for her is that she felt loved by God in that moment. The point for me was that I was listening to and growing in the Holy Spirit.

IT GETS WILD . . .

"He's not a tame lion"[1] goes through my head when I think of stories like this. I was praying at the altar for people as the gathering was ending. The worship team was still producing a wall of sound. The gathering had been charged with the power of God, and I had a line of people waiting to receive prayer. We were prayed up, charged up, and even hyped up. But none of that matters unless Holy Spirit is authenticating what's happening.

I had already prayed and prophesied over four other people. The presence of God fell on them with physical manifestations, but no verifiable miracles. I knew God was working. They knew God was working. *God* knew He was working. But up to that point, there was nothing to authenticate to the skeptic what He was doing.

Then I prayed for a younger lady. With my eyes open, I saw spiritual words on the other side of her back, kind of floating in the air. "Two years ago." So I looked her in the eye and said, "Two years ago . . . ," not knowing what to say next. Then Holy Spirit took over with the rest: "Two years ago . . . your severe back pain started, and that has affected your nervous system and caused you to lose hair. At the same time, you had major trauma in your marriage and emotional life that is ongoing to this day. The trauma

---

[1] From *Chronicles of Narnia,* about Aslan, the lion, who represents God in the epic story.

is the cause of your physical symptoms too. God wants to heal all of it right now."

As the words fell from my mouth, faith rose in the room. Her back was instantly healed. Then I said, "This is the verification that God wants to heal your nervous system, your hair, your emotions, and your marriage."

Sometimes, we need a tangible down payment to confirm the prophetic and spiritual work that God is doing. All of those things happened for her. When you start leaning in and listening to God's voice, sometimes it gets wild! I can't verify that the intense worship music, the passionate gathering, the emotion in the room had anything to do with how Holy Spirit moved in that moment, but I know this: it didn't hurt! It definitely did not hinder or grieve Him. He wasn't scared of the wild environment. In fact, it felt like, at least, He was at home in it; and, at most, He orchestrated it.

"He's not a tame lion," and, in my experience, sometimes it takes a wild environment to produce wild, supernatural results. Don't shy away from the wild move of God. If God's moving, lay your pride down and get in on it. God will speak to you there.

_____

DISCUSS/REFLECT

There were 2 ways that God spoke to me in the wild environment: (1) through an eyes-open vision and (2) through filling my mouth with His words *after* I began to speak in obedience.

When have you experienced a wild environment with God? Has He spoken to you in any ways you weren't prepared for?

_____

_____

_____

_____

_____

What is your next step in developing the habit of hearing God's voice?

_____

_____

_____

_____

What new ways of hearing do you want to explore with Him next?

_____

_____

_____

_____

_____

_____

STUDY

Read Mark 9:2–9 (The Transfiguration). How many different ways does God communicate in these verses?

_____

_____

_____

What would have happened if the disciples didn't follow Jesus's leading to go up the mountain with Him? Or what if they ran away at the sight of Jesus, the cloud, or the voice?

_____

_____

_____

Did their lack of understanding in those moments hinder God's effectiveness?

_____

Why did Jesus tell them to keep it a secret? Are we always ready for what God wants to say?

_____

_____

_____

How can you become more ready and more eager to hear God's voice?

_____

_____

_____

_____

EXERCISE

Take 24 hours to focus on hearing God's voice. Intentionally write down anything and everything that might possibly be God communicating. Ask God about every sensation: *Is that You? What are You saying through it? What else do You want to tell me about it?*

Pray this: "God, I believe that You want to talk to me. Help me to want to listen more. Help me to tune in to Your voice. I want to develop the habit of hearing You, in Jesus name."

Chapter 5 –
Getting My Limb Sawed Off

My face was flush, skin-crawling. Embarrassment began to overwhelm my senses. I was weird, or wrong, or both. Maybe I'd get fired, or an angry mob would come after me with stones.

Rewind a few minutes. I had pain in my left lung, but it was weird because I could sing through it (I was leading worship at the time). The pain felt otherworldly, and I had the same pain the previous week, at the same time. Just as I was getting annoyed by it again, I sensed the nudging of the Holt Spirit: "Call it out."

I had heard of people having pains in their body that represented someone else's pain who needed to get healed, but it had never happened to me. It sounded weird. I didn't want to be weird.

But I was annoyed, so I called it out anyway. "Is there anyone having pain in the left side of their lung? I feel like God wants to heal it." (crickets, except for the awkward strumming of my guitar). I wanted to correct it. Maybe it was just the left side of their body. Or maybe, just maybe, I missed it - *AAAHHHHHH!*

Dun, dun, dunnn. This was my worst nightmare. No one responded in a room of 80 people or so at our Sunday night service. So, I sheepishly moved on. *Quick, sing another song. Does anyone else have a word from God? Is the earth going to swallow me up now?*

I felt so weird in that moment, but, actually, it wasn't weird to the people in the congregation. They just kept worshipping, experiencing God, and giving no attention to the existential crisis their worship leader/kids' pastor was having. My insecurities and fears were almost overwhelming, when truly the worst thing that would have happened was someone might come to me afterward and say, "Did anyone respond to that word about the lung?" And I would say super-spiritually, "Not yet, but I'm believing they will."

I was new to stepping out in faith for the supernatural—passionate, but new. My understanding was limited by my experience. So many in the church today are passionate to see God do what only He can do. There is a drive among many believers that God would show up, that we wouldn't do "normal" Christian life or church. But, just like me, there is often a disconnect between our stirring and our experience.

If you're reading this book, it might be that you are longing to see the supernatural works of God in your own life. You're not alone. Research indicates that at least 800 million Christians in the world today are Charismatic/Pentecostal, and a conservative estimate would say that at least 500 million Christians report some miracle story that they've personally experienced.[2]

I was one of those 500 million who had miracle stories of my own at that time, but the itch inside of my heart was persistent. What if there's more? What if miracles are not supposed to be rare?[3] What if Jesus' and the first Christians' experience with the supernatural was always supposed to be the model for the Christian life? What if that's the key to the explosive growth of Christian faith? What if the supernatural could become normal in my life?

That pursuit metastasized in me (in the best way) so that I could not change the channel. I was digging through the Gospels and Acts daily, praying for any and every condition. God gave me willingness to look stupid in front of my church to see if anyone had pain in their left lung. Then the limb I was climbing out on got sawed off, and I was devastated, but only for a few minutes.

The worship time ended. I began to slink off the stage, and as I did, I heard loudly and quickly the sound of huge footsteps. I was sure it was the angry mob coming to stone me. But it was my drummer, Roger. Roger wasn't my normal drummer. He owned a gym, was about 6'2", 250 lbs. He was very busy, but every once in

---

[2] Keener, Craig. *Miracles: 2 Volumes: The Credibility of the New Testament Accounts*. Location 4988. Grand Rapids: Baker, 2011. Kindle.

[3] Lewis, C.S.. *Miracles (Collected Letters of C.S. Lewis)*. Page 274. New York: HarperCollins, 1947. Kindle.

a while he would step in to play with me, as he had the past 2 weeks.

There he was, towering over me, passionate beyond belief, and he said, "That's me! It's my left lung!" He proceeded to remind me of his motorcycle accident 2 years earlier. What I didn't know is that his left lung had detached in the accident, causing him daily pain if he tried to breathe deeply at all.

We prayed together. Holy Spirit descended and healed his lung on the spot. For the first time in two years, he was breathing without pain!

I don't know if I was more excited about the healing or that I hadn't missed it. (Don't judge. You'd have been excited too!). Holy Spirit confirmed my conviction. He was a little late (as if He could be late). He has a flare for the dramatic sometimes.

In retrospect, of all the happenings in that Sunday night service, God healing Roger's lung was the least weird. It felt right. The Holy Spirit rose up in me. *Was this what it felt like the first time the 72 disciples went out and healed people? What does it mean to do it like the first Christians? Is the supernatural supposed to be a normal part of the Christian life?*

There were so many thoughts and attitudes that needed to shift in me to move this from passion to reality.

DISCUSS/REFLECT

When were you stirred to step out in faith to do something supernatural for the first time? Were there insecurities? What has God taught you?

_____

_____

What *IS* the "normal" Christian life? What *SHOULD* it be?

_____

_____

_____

_____

STUDY

Read Luke chapter 10 (Jesus Sends the 72). Ask Jesus to speak to you as you read.

What stood out to you as you read? What stirred in your spirit? How did God speak to you?

_____

_____

_____

_____

_____

There was no contemporary precedent for what these disciples experienced. Are there specific things Jesus might call you to right now that would be out of your comfort zone?

_____

_____

_____

_____

_____

EXERCISE

Ask God to do something specific that He's never done through you before. Write down your prayer:

_____

_____

_____

_____

_____

_____

_____

_____

_____

_____

_____

Section 2:

Quick Start Guide

Tips for risking and acting in faith right now (which you should)

Chapter 6 –
Be Opportunistic

When I started becoming excited about incurable illnesses, chronic conditions, visible afflictions, and constant pain, I began to wonder if my compassion-meter was broken. Some of you are thinking emphatically that it is. (I know it's you, Judgy McJudger.) Just hear me out. As I began to pray for people more in Jesus' name, not giving up but leaning in deeper every time, I learned that I couldn't break anything. I began to realize that every illness that didn't not get healed was simply what would have happened anyway. My prayers didn't make the person sicker. I found that even absent a healing, people felt loved when my heart was in the right place.

Then the epiphany: There is no downside to praying for healing! I can pray for *everyone!* If people don't get healed, they can still feel loved. When people *do* get healed . . . *JESUS!* So, be opportunistic. Go after every opportunity to pray for healing.

That's why I get excited after hearing about sickness. I *know* it's an opportunity for Jesus to receive glory. The illness would happen whether I'm involved or not, but because I'm involved, I have the occasion to pair Holy Spirit who dwells in me with this impossibility.

SEE THE MIRACLE

First, we must recognize an opportunity to pray for a miracle for someone before we can seize it. As a children's pastor, I no longer had the luxury to see band aids and sick pets as cute anecdotes or humorous stories to share over lunch with other pastors at Chick-Fil-A. I began to see them as opportunities to raise the tide of faith in the child, the parent, everyone wandering by, and the church at large.

Every time I pray for these seemingly insignificant needs (and other, more apparent ones), I see the true significance of every God-given opportunity to build faith in individuals.

With each prayer, I fully intend to "get their hopes up," not so that they can be dashed but so those desires can be fulfilled. The healing of a paper cut certainly won't make it onto CBN or into *Charisma* magazine, but it will plant a seed in a child's heart that, "Nothing is impossible with God," and that He cares about their every thought and need (Luke 1:37).

Children will come with the same simple faith when the doctor tells them they have cancer as they did when Fluffy was sick; except this time, they've seen God move before. They will astound their parents with spiritual maturity, grace, and authority in those moments because a spiritual leader planted the seed of faith and decided to be opportunistic and risked looking foolish for God.

Thousands of holy men had likely passed by the blind man throughout the thirty-eight years that he sat begging before Jesus saw him (John 9:1). Seeing an opportunity for a miracle is more of the battle than many believers know. Christians all have miracle opportunities sitting in their churches, taking walks in their neighborhood, and passing by at the grocery store. The faith in our church context has risen to the point that when I hear, "Our son was diagnosed with a chromosomal abnormality," my spirit leaps because I know that God has brought another opportunity for Him to receive glory. We need to see the miracle with eyes of faith before they can see the miracle that God performs.

HEAR THE MIRACLE

Remember my testimony about hearing a crying baby in my spirit while my wife was in the operating room, followed by the literal, physical sound of my newborn son crying. There was no surprise, shock or awe at some medical miracle. Instead, only praise arose for my God, because my boy was alive.

Christians have to hear miracles ringing in their spirits before they watch God do them. They need to recognize the voice of God directing them, keep their prayer language sharp, and listen for the prophetic assurance that God is doing the work. Believers will have the opportunity to draw a line in the sand between life and death for the people around them as they faithfully listen to the soundings of God's Spirit.

We cannot share prophetic words in proper timing if we are not hearing them first. Hearing the miracle will be a directive function before we see the miracle—a prophetic unction as we pray for the miracle. It's an assurance of the victory before it comes. It all starts with listening well.

DISCUSS/REFLECT

Where do you regularly see and hear people's needs? What is your present response to needs? How can you respond more like Christ?

_____

_____

_____

_____

How can you create more opportunities to see and hear needs?

_____

_____

_____

_____

_____

STUDY

Read Exodus 4:1–9 (Moses practicing miracles). Ask Jesus to speak to you as you read.

What stood out to you as you read? What stirred in your spirit? How did God speak to you?

_____

_____

_____

_____

_____

_____

Why did God speak to Moses and have him practice these miracles?

_____

_____

_____

_____

_____

How can you begin to see the miracle and hear the miracle ahead of time in your prayer life like Moses?

_____

_____

_____

_____

_____

_____

EXERCISE

Ask God who you need to see right now and what impossible thing you can pray for them, then write down your prayer.

_____

_____

_____

_____

_____

Chapter 7 –
Stepping out

The temptation to hesitate is real. Anytime the opportunity to do something for God arises, we naturally find a myriad of excuses. Here are two keys to dispel excuses and get into action: Lower the bar & Embrace the MUMs (Mildly Uncomfortable Moments).

LOWER THE BAR

I have a tinge of perfectionist in me. From the time I was first told I could hear God's voice as a kid, I started listening consistently for God's voice—in some seasons, daily. I'd just sit there, thinking, trying to clear my mind, straining to hear something, and nothing. I didn't know how to confirm God's voice. I didn't know if what I was thinking was actually God. With stubborn tenacity, I refused to make it up or get it wrong.

Drew Neal said that most seasoned Christians have an attitude of "it's probably me, but it might be God" when it comes to hearing God's voice. If that's your attitude, eventually you will find yourself frustrated in hearing God's voice and even lost when it comes to daily meaningful interactions with God.

Drew recommended shifting that attitude to, "it's probably God, but it might be me."[4] I agree. Obviously, you never want to get so arrogant that you're beyond weighing and testing God's words all the time. Yet, lowering the bar even that little bit, with that subtle shift in attitude, will open up a consistency and regularity in hearing God's voice that is necessary for ongoing relationship. So, lower the bar, test the words constantly, and give yourself permission to fail.

Many ministers are quite impressed with themselves when they have 100% accuracy or even 90% accuracy in words of knowledge. But the key to a regular rhythm of hearing God's voice for the growing Christian is giving yourself permission to hit 60% during some seasons of life, testing the words more often, and then following the ways of hearing God's voice that prove accurate.

For example, suppose I'm at Burger King and have a random thought about the cashier that her daughter's sick. If my attitude is "it's probably me," then I'll just ignore it. However, if my attitude

---

[4] Neal, Drew. "Solutionary." Lecture, Journey Life Church, Holt, MI, October 13, 2019.

is "it's probably God," then I'll want to test it. Then, when it's my turn in line, I'll ask, "Hey, do you have a daughter?" If the answer is yes, then I'll say something like, "I'm learning to hear God's voice right now, and I felt like He told me you have a daughter and she needs prayer right now." Then ask to pray for her. If you find out in the course of conversation that she is sick, then that's further confirmation, that you're hearing correctly.

Now, if the answer to, "Do you have a daughter?" is, "No," then, you move on, order your food, and get into your quiet time with the Lord and ask, "God, how can I hear You clearer? What is a better way of listening?" Recalibrate with the Lord in that moment.

The disciples did this in Matthew 17:14–21 after they failed to drive out a demon from a boy. They came to Jesus on their own and asked, "Why couldn't we drive it out?" Jesus took the time to teach them, and the Holy Spirit will definitely do the same with you. This is one of the essential paths to growth in the supernatural—allowing the Holy Spirit opportunities to teach you when you fail.

The tendency for many Christians when they fail at hearing God's voice is to:

1. Back away from listening to God's voice, because they assume they just don't have the gift (if they're ignorant).
2. Explain it away as some future-fulfillment prophetic mumbo-jumbo (if they're arrogant).

3. Blame it on God's will (if they're arrogant and/or ignorant).

The first response of backing away from listening to God's voice is ignorant because you don't understand what being in an apprenticeship with the Holy Spirit means. It means that you will fail sometimes. You have to fail in order to ask the right questions, learn, and grow.

Explaining it away is often the response of those who have staked their reputation in some way on accuracy in hearing God's voice. These people are trying to save face and want to appear spiritual in front of others.

Blaming it on God's will is the response of those whose theological presuppositions prevent them from imagining a world in which God's will is not always completely done. However, the Bible is quite clear that we need to pray for God's will to be done and that "the prince of the kingdom of the air" (Eph 2:2) still has quite a lot of influence here.

The proper response, again, is to mimic the disciples, get alone with the Lord, submit yourself to His mentorship, and ask good questions. I promise He will help you grow. The range of responses I've received from Him in these moments include …

- "I needed to spend time with you, thank you for this time."

- "Here's a totally different area of your life I'd like to work on…"

- "I love that you're listening. Keep listening."
- "This is what my voice sounds like…"
- "Stop listening in that way for now."

All of these were helpful and encouraging. The Holy Spirit will always point you to your next step in Him in some way. So, lower the bar, test the words, and give the Holy Spirit room to grow you.

EMBRACE THE MUMS
(MILDLY UNCOMFORTABLE MOMENTS)

The blood started to drain from my face. I had met him probably three times before but couldn't remember his name. Who knew wandering into the front yard to pull in the garbage can could turn into an emotional and existential crisis!

Awkward smile. "Hey . . . man." What a travesty! How embarrassing to not even know my next-door neighbor's first name. You may be able to relate.

Then God inspired Jessica and I to get serious about neighboring. After living in the same neighborhood for 2.5 years, we finally got intentional about it. (Full disclosure: we quickly reached for the book *The Art Of Neighboring,* which I highly recommend). We realized that "Loving Our Neighbor 101" meant learning everyone in our neighborhood's names. So, over the next 5 months, I had this conversation many, many times, "Hey I know

I met you before, but honestly I forgot you name. Remind me your name." Awkward. Uncomfortable. But worth it.

In just 5 months for me, "Hey . . . man" became, "Hey, Ryan," then, "Hey, Ryan, how was your week?" to, "Hey, Ryan, how's your daughter liking her new school?" to "Hey, Ryan, you and the family should come over and join us for dinner this week." And that has become, "Hey, Ryan, what can I pray for you about?" Now I am positioned properly in this person's life to command healing into their body or to give them what I feel might be a word from God. Because, whether or not they get healed, or whether the word is dead on, they know that I love them as their neighbor first.

So many believers stunt their own growth in faith, evangelism, character, and the supernatural because we're unwilling to embrace Mildly Uncomfortable Moments. Here's the reality: When you embrace the MUMs, they'll soon disappear. Those strangers who live all around you will become neighbors— neighbors who you can love, neighbors who have real issues and real passions, real strengths to offer, and real value to God. And you'll find they'll have real value to you to.

So many of us have made unconscious commitments to unhealthy relationships because we're not willing to step out of our comfort zones and embrace enough mildly uncomfortable moments to have healthy ones. Practice at church. Praying for someone at church is only mildly uncomfortable. There's a huge chance that these people are totally on board.

The commitment to embrace mildly uncomfortable moments also leads to more and more comfortability in those moments. In fact, it becomes very fun. You start to get to know your waiter, joke with them, call them by name, before you say, "Hey, I'm a Christian, I'm learning to hear God's voice, and I feel like He told me that you have pain in your right shoulder. He only tells me that, when He wants to heal it . . ."

DISCUSS/REFLECT

Do you have perfectionist tendencies when you listen for God's voice? What's the worst that can happen if you hear wrong? What's the best?

_____

_____

_____

_____

_____

When was the last time you asked someone's name that you should have remembered? How can you use mildly uncomfortable moments to your advantage as a Christian?

_____

_____

_____

_____

_____

STUDY

Read Acts 3:1–10 (Peter, John & the crippled beggar). In what ways was the initial situation uncomfortable for Peter and John?

_____

_____

_____

Do you think the apostles were 100% certain that this man would be healed when they went to pray for him? Would you have been?

_____

Would you have commanded the man, "Look at us!" (Verse 4)? Why do you think Peter did that, knowing he didn't have any money? What's the worst that could have happened to them?

_____

_____

_____

EXERCISE

Write down a list of mildly uncomfortable moments that you face throughout your day.

_____

_____

_____

_____

_____

_____

Chapter 8 –
Nothing's Too Small for God

I was being crushed. Even though I was in the middle of the thrilling season when God was first breaking open for me practical truths about the supernatural, this day was Struggle-City.

I had been stuck in a mess in my head, feeling down about my spiritual life—shadow boxing with people and situations in my life who I guarantee had not given me a second thought.

I was traveling upstairs to my office with my hands full of knick-knacks and weird randomness that you sometimes have to carry. I had over-packed my arms and was ready to drop everything, on my way to a door that was always locked.

Then a familiar sound came. It was familiar, but I hadn't heard it in long enough that it was startling and almost unnerving. It was the still small voice of God's Spirit. He said, "Jared, don't try to get your keys out. I've got this."

Out of mostly exhaustion and curiosity, I obeyed and just pushed on the door. To my surprise, it opened. I stumbled into my office, dumped all my stuff on the desk, collapsed in a chair, and melted before my God. *God, why are You so good to me? Why would you care enough about me to break through in this moment, speaking my language, overwhelming me with love?*

Those thoughts dominated my times with God for weeks, and God began to show me some of these truths as it got emblazoned in my soul—the truth that "Nothing's too small for God." Nothing's too insignificant that it will not fall into His purview. Nothing is too underwhelming that God can't find wonder in it. Nothing is boring when God is active in your life. No one can find a spot in God's world where God hasn't created something amazing, awe-filled, creative, beautiful, wonderful, and noble. Nothing is too small for God.

Satan is fixated on the details of evil, highlighting our mistakes, sins, and troubles. God, however, is fixated on life, truth, and the expression of that life and truth in us. Most of us have the two voices mixed up, and our broken misconceptions have made us partner with Satan. We've given him that stronghold in our minds. He works fear, shame, and disappointment thoroughly into our mindsets, and then he blames it on God.

The mind of Christ in us is fixated on majesty, wonder, creativity, nobility, and so on. What does it mean to be fixated on majesty, wonder, creativity, and nobility? It means that we develop the ability to reframe everything and everyone in our lives in light of God's mindset. It means we think about the things God thinks about.

With this mindset, we are excited even when God heals little things. We focus on those little things, talk about them, wonder about how awesome God is that He would also care about that. It means that we look for and find little confirmations of God's activity.

IT'S THE LITTLE THINGS...

Don't expect God's activity to slap you upside the head every time. He only spoke through a donkey once and parted the sea once. But there are amazing confirmations of God's activity every day. "Oh, that was in August." "Oh, that was last year." But wait! We serve a God who is the same yesterday, today, and forever. Fixate on His goodness. Fixate on His wonder. If He has ever said, or done, or spoken, or confirmed, or healed, or energized you in the past, live in that place. That's your "new person." You are that new creation! Luke 16:10 says, "Whoever can be trusted with very little can also be trusted with much, and whoever is dishonest with very little will also be dishonest with much." Steward the little move of God.

The new creation leans into the mind of Christ and does "little acts of awesome" to the people around us. We give little bits of heaven away, as though heaven were our home (because it is).

When we see something that doesn't look like our home—heaven—we don't complain or fixate or ruminate on it; we address it until it either does look like heaven or time expires on our opportunity. In many cases, we pass that opportunity on to another Spirit-inspired believer who also will address it until it looks like heaven.

Fixating on majesty, wonder, creativity, and nobility looks like hearing God in unlikely ways. If God only spoke in likely ways, we wouldn't realize it was Him. We would try to harness and manipulate those ways, turning them into methods we can control. We need to listen for God's voice in new ways and look for His activity in new places.

"Why isn't God speaking to me anymore?" He is; it's just that He's doing it differently now. "I used to hear His still small voice in my spirit and now not anymore." What if He wants to show you things in dreams or visons—pictures and moving pictures—or through "coincidences," or through your pastor, or some non-believer at work, or some random street sign. Maybe He's speaking through an open door or a closed door, or through the Bible, or through your worship leader. Maybe God didn't stop speaking. Maybe He's simply interested in you growing in listening. Maybe He's less interested in your comfortable way of hearing Him than He is in your overall spiritual development and your becoming who He has called you to be.

Matthew tells us an amazing little story:

"When Jesus came into Peter's house, he saw Peter's mother-in-law lying in bed with a fever. He touched her hand and the fever left her, and she got up and began to wait on him. When evening came, many who were demon-possessed were brought to him, and he drove out the spirits with a word and healed all the sick. This was to fulfill what was spoken through the prophet Isaiah: "He took up our infirmities and bore our diseases." (Matt 8:14-17)

This was not a major healing. It was a fever that broke. But do you see Peter's mother-in-law's response? She got up and went to work. She stewarded the move of God with her gratitude. Also, obviously, everyone around went and told the whole town about the "little" miracle. What were they doing? They were stewarding God's move.

The little miracle of a fever breaking started a healing revival in the town. We could call it the fever revival. How many of us are ready to start a fever revival? How many of us are ready to be the person who got healed of a fever and immediately set to work, serving in gratitude?

Anything in God's hands is major. Anything in God's hands can start a revival. The question is, are we ready to change our perspective and see God's activity like He does? Are you ready to be a sign of God's activity? Are you ready to start a fever revival?

Don't even get me started on the dysentery revival that Paul started on Malta! Are you ready to be a sign of God's activity?

Is anything too small for God? If we believe that answer to be "no"—if we believe that nothing is too small for God—then we're ready to start talking about His work, His goodness, and His movement in our lives.

What if God is concerned about what we're concerned about? What if He cares simply because we care? 1 Peter 5:7 says, "Cast all your anxiety on him because he cares for you." And what if, at the same time, God is endeavoring to steer our concerns toward "little" things that are really big in His eyes?

What are the little things that we need to begin to care about in our world? Our patterns of thought. The simple needs of those around us. The various situations where God can show up and show off. If we aren't ever concerned enough to show God's power in the little things, how is it that we have the audacity to demand He show up in the big ones?

What little decisions do we need to give God jurisdiction to mess with?

Is God really concerned about my sock drawer? You'd be surprised. God can use a fever or dysentery to start a revival. He can use a seed to move a mountain. He can do more with your sock-level decisions than you think.

What if God sometimes reminds us of insignificant things that will put us on a path toward His big purposes? Why did I just think of that home on my street where the owner can never seem to mow his lawn? Do you even know those neighbors? Have you thought this might be an opportunity to show them what love looks like?

We might miss God's little nudges for a while, but eventually He's going to win. God is going to show us His good purposes in the details of our lives. He created us with those details. They are there for a purpose. And in God's hands, they will form us into the image of beauty, majesty, wonder, creativity and nobility.

Then you say things like, "I'll be glad when this is over," you're delaying your gladness. "I'll be glad when this is over" means you can't be glad *until* it's over. But even when it's over, most likely you won't be glad because you'll already be focused on the next problem. Change the way you speak about struggles. Rejoice now, before the answer comes.

Or, what about, "I'll be glad, when this happens"? What if it's not going to happen until you're glad? There is a place of joy in God that is completely separate from our earthly condition. There is a nourishing presence of God that is not dependent on our circumstances but instead has the power to literally change them.

No God-activity is insignificant. Our small things become huge in God's hands.

God understands our details so much, especially when it comes to our devotional lives—our prayer, worship, and Bible reading in personal time before God. These are our personal acts of devotion. God understands the balance we need between familiarity with His presence and new experiences with Him. And He's infinite, so He's always able to give us something new.

God is a master at pushing the correct amounts of familiarity versus novelty into our lives. It is a dance. We just have to get on the same page with our Father and begin to dance with Him, rather than stepping on His toes all the time.

When we grow so comfortable that we slip into negative habits, thought patterns, and sin, He will push us into unfamiliar waters where the old patterns don't work anymore. If we respond in these seasons with mistrust and discomfort rather than curiosity and excitement, we're missing the point.

There are times to lean into the familiar paths in our relationships with God. Jeremiah 6:16 says, "Ask for the ancient paths, ask where the good way is, and walk in it, and you will find rest for your souls." There are also times to lean into new and unfamiliar paths in our relationships with God, knowing that this is a new wineskin or a patch of unshrunk cloth.

God is a master at leading this dance. Remember all the times that He has changed His cadence with you. Recognize that this is what He has been doing, and begin to move at the pace He's moving.

… Because nothing's too small for God.

DISCUSS/REFLECT

Here's a word from God for you: You're not too small for Him. He cares about what you care about. He thinks huge, majestic, noble, wonder-filled, creative thoughts about you. Learn to see what He sees when He looks at you. It's so much more beautiful and awesome than any picture you've ever had of yourself. God's picture of you has the power to transform you into it His image. Ask Him, "Father, how do you see me?"

Now, reflect on that word from God. What are some specific areas of thought that God is transforming in you?

_____

_____

_____

_____

STUDY

Read Acts 28:7–11 (The Dysentery Revival). Ask Jesus to speak to you as you read.

What stirred in your spirit as you read? How did God speak to you?

_____

_____

_____

_____

After Paul was bitten by the snake and survived, (a big miracle; they worshipped him as a god), no one asked him to pray for them for healing. When did they ask? What does this mean for your prayers?

_____

_____

_____

_____

EXERCISE

Do you believe nothing's too small for God? Do you want to get well? Or do you just like the pity party of feeling bad for yourself? Shift your mindset right now. Write down every area of your life that you want to be well. Begin to rejoice, and declare His wholeness in your life.

_____

_____

_____

_____

_____

_____

_____

_____

_____

_____

_____

_____

_____

_____

_____

_____

Chapter 9 –

Share Your Faith Story

Whoever believes in the Son of God accepts this [God's] testimony. Whoever does not believe God has made him out to be a liar, because they have not believed the testimony God has given about his Son. And **this is the testimony**: God has given **us** eternal life, and this life is in his Son. (1 John. 5:10–11, emphasis added)

God's story is us. Anyone who has faith in Jesus *is* the testimony about Jesus. Do you see those words in Scripture? "And this is the testimony . . ." God's testimony: eternal life for *us*. That testimony is being heard and read by our world, every day, in *us*. People are looking at you and reading God's story.

If God's story is us, how are we sharing it? The answer is in the quality of what we're sharing: Do we authentically look, act, and feel like Jesus? The answer is also in the quantity: Are we hiding our faith behind work, fear, busyness, or "I just don't feel like I know how to do this"? God wants to break us out of all of that. God's story is *us who believe.*

John wrote, "Whoever has the Son has life; whoever does not have the Son of God does not have life" (1 John 5:12). The prerequisite to having a faith story to share is spending time with Jesus. Jesus is the author of faith, and He's the One who makes faith whole too—the fulfiller of our faith (Heb. 12:2). Without Him, our faith is nothing.

Growing faith depends on spending time with Jesus. If you've spent time with Jesus before, it's time to remember how awesome that is and commit to spending time with Him some more. Maybe you need to be reintroduced to Him. Jesus wants to give you life.

GOD'S STORY . . .

God's story is life-giving. You might have met some life-sucking Christians before. I promise, none of that flows from God's story. God's story is life-giving. He shows us how to live life with purpose and significance. He shows us how to live life with joy, and to live our best earthly life (this side of eternity) right now—not some fake, masked substitute. God calls us up to something better and empowers us to become it.

God's story is certain. You can know for sure whether you're going to heaven. If you don't yet, you need to. Talk to God and clear that up right now. God's story is certain. We either know that, or we don't. As John noted, "I write these things to you who believe in the name of the Son of God so that you may know that you have eternal life. This is the confidence we have in approaching God: that if we ask anything according to his will, he hears us. And if we know that he hears us—whatever we ask—we know that we have what we asked of him" (1 John. 5:13–15).

God's story is obvious. Prayers offered by believing believers produce supernatural results. The supernatural is normal in God's story. We experience it every week at church. God's story is authentic and obvious. We are who we are. I've seen God do some crazy good things. God's story is obvious, and it's going to become more and more obvious to all of us.

TELL THE STORY

Until you share your faith story, you haven't seen the full benefits from it. There are tons of Bible stories that show this, but just take it from my son.

You know how when kids are certain ages, you can measure how bad the scream is going to be by how long it takes them, with open mouth, to fill up with air before the scream? The longer the fill-up, the louder and longer the scream. My son Jaren was 5 years old. He had bonked his head hard on the way out of church one Wednesday night, and the silence before the scream was happening, so I grabbed him in my arms and then planted him on his car seat, because we were right there. And then, the scream. And then, about a golf-ball-sized bump on his head.

Jaren and I had been talking about healing a lot, and as soon as the scream died down soft enough for him to hear me, I said, "Let's pray for it—right now. Jesus is going to heal your bump. Do you feel how big it is?"

"Yeah," he replied

"It's huge isn't it?"

"Yeah."

"Let's pray."

So we prayed, and we felt like the bump might have gone down a little. But the screaming—*that* went down a lot. God was healing his pain.

So, we prayed again. All in the space of less than a minute, the bump went down a lot. Then I backed off, and he prayed, Suddenly, the bump was completely gone. Less than a minute. That's miraculous. Later, my son could not stop jumping up and down and telling people about what God had done on his head. That's sharing your faith story, and that's what paves the way for more.

What if Jaren held that story inside and didn't tell anyone about it? He wouldn't experience the euphoria of joy from others toward him. He wouldn't even have fully sealed up the remembrance of that story for the future.

Jaren was only five years old. Do you think he remembers that experience now? He certainly does! Maybe not the screaming, but he remembers what God did. There's a childlikeness to faith that reaps the full benefits of faith, not just for you, but for everyone around you.

Until we share our faith stories, we haven't cleared out room for more. We're meant to be rivers, not reservoirs. Everything we receive must go out.

It's healthy when you remember your faith stories, but it's even better for you and the atmosphere around you when you share them. All of you have experienced this. All of you have had bummer conversations turned around by one hope-filled story. It goes the opposite way too. A story can be sad in some of the results and still produce hope in the room when you tell it in light of true, authentic faith.

Let me demonstrate: "My friend died way too soon. He was a good man. He will be missed." That's fine. That's a decent grieving statement. But what if it was said this way: "My friend died way too soon. He was a person of faith, and he's with Jesus now. He'll be missed until I see him again. I'm sure he doesn't want to come back. He's having crazy fun right now in heaven!" Same content, same grieving, but there's hope. There's joy.

Jesus came to earth and then went to the cross so that we can have that kind of hope and joy. Tell your story from a place of hope and victory in Christ.

THE POWER OF YOUR STORY

Testimony charges the spiritual realm with hope. It charges our souls. It charges up the people around us. And think about this: it charges up the supernatural activity—the angels and Holy Spirit—so now we're inviting more, because God is getting glory from us.

Along those lines, **testimony increases the probability of the supernatural for everyone who hears.** This is why there are hotbeds for miracles. This is why certain places and people are seeing God do outrageously good things more and more. If we hesitate to talk about what God has done, how can we expect Him to do more?

Through testimony, the tide of faith rises in a community, and everyone experiences God more.

Here are 3 more points worth meditating on, but I'm going to share them quickly for the sake of time.

- **Testimony puts action to faith.**
- **Testimony strengthens our faith.**
- **Testimony is a cry to God to do it again.**

MY FAITH STORY: AN EXAMPLE

I'm a pastors kid who never had a reason to rebel. I got ruined in the best way as a kid, seeing God do outrageously good, supernatural things. My grandpa was a first-generation believer and broke the curses from my family, so I grew up in the blessing of his obedience. Some of you have the opportunity to be that person for your own families.

My faith story also includes a bunch of other faith stories, like how in the last decade, I've seen God do thousands of miracles. Why? Because God is awesome, and He loves us. He thinks we're amazing, and He's always ready to rock our world with goodness. If God has done it for me, He wants to do it for you too. As I share my faith story, I'm crying out for God to do it again.

Our words produce. **Our problem becomes a faith story— a testimony—at the moment we commit to God to journey forward through it.** Some of us are stuck in situations longer than we need to be because we're not willing to commit, with our words and attitudes, to God's plan. Start telling your story even now, and watch what God does.

DISCUSS/REFLECT

What's your faith story? Who were you before Jesus? Who was instrumental in bringing you to Jesus? How did things change after you met Jesus?

_____

_____

_____

_____

_____

_____

What are other stories of God's goodness in your life? List as many as possible.

_____

_____

_____

_____

_____

_____

_____

_____

_____

STUDY

Read Acts 3:8-12 (Aftermath of cripple healing). Ask Jesus to speak to you as you read.

What stirred in your spirit as you read? How did God speak to you?

_____

_____

_____

_____

_____

Did the cripple have perfectly refined words for this moment? How did people respond to the former cripple's jumping and praising?

_____

_____

_____

_____

_____

EXERCISE

Tell someone one of your faith stories right now. Call or text someone, or walk to their house and knock on the door. Put faith to action right now. Simply tell them you want to encourage them with a story. Perhaps then ask if you can pray for them.

Chapter 10 –
Raise the Tide of Faith

The kiddie pool is very fun . . . for kids. But for a teenager, sitting on the edge of the kiddie pool, bored out of their mind, is a terribly sad sight. They need deeper waters.

You need deeper waters in your faith too. There are ways for a community of believers to raise the tide of faith for everyone. There are ways for an entire community to wade into the deeper waters that require more faith, which is rewarded with more fun and more breakthrough as well. The following tools will help raise the tide of faith.

CELEBRATE WITHOUT JEALOUSY

"When Elizabeth heard Mary's greeting, the baby leaped in her womb, and Elizabeth was filled with the Holy Spirit" (Luke 1:41). Elizabeth would likely not have naturally known Mary's voice. It had been years since they saw each other. Elizabeth heard

Mary's voice, and the Holy Spirit caused John to jump (this is a word that can be translated "skipping!"). So John is dancing a jig inside of Elizabeth, Elizabeth is overwhelmed with the feeling of Holy Spirit working in her, and immediately, she prophesies—immediately, she speaks words of life over Mary and her baby. Now, don't you think Mary made the right choice in going to see Elizabeth?

Who we are choosing to hang around will determine the words that are spoken over us. That's why it's important to be in church and to "do life" with people who are looking to build up our souls. Doing life with people who are willing and ready to call out God's gold in us will raise the tide of faith.

Look at Elizabeth's prophecy: "Blessed are you among women, and blessed is the child you will bear! But why am I so favored, that the mother of my Lord should come to me?" (Luke 1:42–43).

Did Elizabeth know that Mary was pregnant? Not likely. Mary barely knew that Mary was pregnant. There were no text messages or emails to bring the news before Mary's arrival. God showed Elizabeth. That's a word of knowledge.

Now think about this: Elizabeth not only immediately knew that Mary was pregnant, but she immediately knew that Mary's miraculous baby was way more important than her own miraculous baby. And she celebrated with her! There was zero jealousy—complete celebration. Why? Because Elizabeth realized God's plan was bigger than her. When you celebrate the supernatural work of

God without jealousy, you will raise the tide of faith for your community.

GET YOUR HOPE UP

I have a confession to make. I get people's hopes up. That's what I do. Not so that they can be dashed but so that they can be realized, fulfilled, and expanded. "Now hope does not disappoint, because the love of God has been poured out in our hearts by the Holy Spirit who was given to us." (Romans 5:5, NKJV).

I have another confession to make. My daughter Jemma was four when her finger got caught in the hinge of a self-closing door, and her fingernail cracked in half horizontally, with the back end of the nail sitting on top of the cuticle. It was bleeding directly through the center of the nail, every time we dabbed blood away, it would come back up straight along that line. I gave her the idea to believe for the nail to be healed. I got her hopes up. I filled her head with hope—not because I'm anything great, but because Jesus has filled me with hope.

We put the finger in a splint and began to believe God for complete healing—that the nail itself would mend, which is impossible. We've had five x-rays on this thing now. One of them showed a break in the bone through the growth plate. The next one didn't! Why would that be? A fingernail that is cracked does not mend back together; it just grows out. It's medically impossible for a finger to mend to itself again—there is only dead tissue there.

It's like asking for hair that is cut to become uncut. But do you know that nothing is impossible with God? What if we became aware of this heavenly reality more and more?

Jemma's fingernail has mended back together. Our God delights in defying impossibilities. Is this a super-consequential miracle, as far as natural consequences? Not really. I could think of a ton of people who need the impossible way more than her finger. But it matters. Why? Because when heaven shows up, it *always* matters. There actually are no inconsequential miracles. Every time God shows up and shows off, He's giving a joy that can never be taken away. Twenty years from now, we can think back on this moment, and we can know that God, beyond any doubt, was here. We can be filled with that same joy all over again.

That's why I'm on a mission to get people's hope up. "Well, I don't want to get my hopes up." Too bad. God does. When hope raises, so does the possibility for God's supernatural intervention.

DON'T CHANGE THE CHANNEL

Hope is forward-looking. Hope restores. Hope itself restores us. As Christians, we aren't people who passively need to have our hope restored. No. We have a never-ending spring of hope in the person of Jesus Christ. That hope restores us. So many Christians are waiting constantly for their hope to be restored, when all they have to do is look at Jesus.

Jesus is the hope of the world. Hope for today, hope for tomorrow, hope for the near future, hope for the far future, hope for eternity. You know: eternity—the thing that's already written on our hearts as believers. It's already written. We've already entered into eternity (John 17:3).

People often ask me about how I'm seeing miracles and healings through prayer at the rate we are. I have to point this out: I wasn't always seeing miracles at this rate, but I decided (before I began seeing miracles at any rate) that the hope in Jesus's power and ability in my life was worth renewing daily. So, I began to focus on what God had done in me and not on what specifically I wasn't yet seeing. I decided not to change the channel and simply continue to believe that God has the power to heal. No matter how many snotty noses I prayed for that stayed snotty, I wasn't changing the channel. No matter how many toe fungi I prayed for that stayed fungi-y—no matter how many sprained ankles, or allergies, or headaches, or cancers, or liver problems, or asthma's, or diabetes, arthritis, or crones, or *you fill in the blank*—I prayed for all of them.

But there came a shift in my thinking where it didn't matter when it didn't happen. I would still get excited about the next opportunity to give God maximum glory. I would remind myself that there were a few times that I saw God do it. I would remind myself of God's word that says it's His will to heal. And in those ways, I would tap into a fresh stream of hope. Every problem that presents itself to the believer has a better promise from God attached to it. And if the promise is that big and awesome, can you imagine how wonderful the answer will be?

That dogged determination in my heart—my unwillingness to change the channel, praying for any and every need I could find—I believe became the seeds for the breakthroughs we've now seen. Keep praying for everyone, visibly and verbally. It will raise the tide of faith.

Discuss/Reflect

Have you allowed your hope to sag at times? Has disappointment ever hijacked your hope? How can you recommit to hope today?

_____

_____

_____

_____

_____

Have you ever prayed for someone who didn't get healed? How did you react? How can you react differently? How can you commit fully to hope?

_____

_____

_____

_____

_____

STUDY

Read Luke 1:36, 39–45 (Mary & Elizabeth). Ask Jesus to speak to you as you read.

What stirred in your spirit as you read? How did God speak to you?

_____

_____

_____

_____

_____

Why was Elizabeth the perfect person for Mary to visit in this moment? How did Elizabeth encourage Mary in her miracle?

_____

_____

_____

_____

_____

EXERCISE

Celebrate someone in your life right now who's seen a miracle. Also, pray for someone right now who needs a miracle. Find them. Scour social media if you have to. Then message them a specific, faith-filled prayer.

Section 3:

Because, the Bible . . .

Biblical Foundations

Chapter 11 –

Pray Like Jesus

Jesus's prayer life was incredible. What would it have been like if we had been with Him on that mountain at that special place of prayer that He went to usually—normally? Can you even imagine the conversation that God the Son had with God the Father? The levels of revelation and vision and breakthrough and love that must have exploded like fireworks in those prayer times?

We don't know a whole lot about the specific content of Jesus's prayer life. We have some major clues about it and a few glimpses into it, and we'll talk about those next. But Jesus prayed differently than we often do. Get ready to be challenged by the prayer life of Jesus.

DISRUPTIVE PRAYER

We know Jesus prayed often, sometimes all night. We know He fasted. We know He saw breakthrough after He prayed. Here is an outline of some of the times Jesus prayed, and the incredibly significant events that immediately followed or preceded . . .

- **Mark 1:35–46** – Jesus prayed and then changed His preaching itinerary entirely. He had all the crowds following Him there, and He left them and ministered elsewhere—preaching, driving out demons, healing.

- **Matthew 3:13–4:11** – Jesus was water baptized, and God affirmed Him in front of everyone for public ministry. Then, immediately, Jesus went into 40 days of prayer, fasting, and temptation, having angels show up. It was a supernatural prayer time with angelic visitation.

- **Mark 6:45–56** – Jesus went to pray, came down from the mountain, walked on water, calmed the storm, and then went across the lake and healed everyone.

- **Luke 6:12–19** – Jesus went to pray. When He came back, He immediately choose the perfect 12 disciples for God's plan. Then He healed everyone who came to Him.

- **John 6:15–69** – After people were going to come after Jesus to try to make Him king by force, He withdrew to pray. Then He immediately preached the "Bread of Life" discourse: "You'll have to eat me" (something like that). Everyone left Him except the 12, and they were tempted to leave too. Jesus was checking His followers' motives. Did they want Him as a person or just His power?

- **Matthew 14:12–21** – John was beheaded, so Jesus went to pray. The crowds found Him anyway. He had compassion on them, healed everyone, and fed 5,000 men (plus women and children).

There are three times in Scripture when the disciples caught a glimpse into Jesus' prayer times. The first one (His temptation in the wilderness), they knew about it because Jesus told them. The next two (His transfiguration and later in Gethsemene), they knew because Jesus invited them along. We have to assume that these were normal prayer times for Jesus. We have nothing else to go on. The disciples assumed this. The authors of Scripture assumed this was normal.

1) THE TEMPTATION

Jesus was minding His own business, fasting in the desert for forty days, and the devil manifested, showing up in person to tempt Him. According to the Scripture, Jesus hadn't done a single miracle yet, but the devil knew it was coming. So the devil tempted Him to use miracles to feed himself. Then Satan tempted Him to use miracles for thrills (jump off this height … see if they'll catch you … it'll be fun). Finally, he tempted Jesus to use miracles to gain hierarchical status, power, and rule. After defeating all three temptations, angels came to Jesus to strengthen Him. Just another time of prayer for Jesus.

2) THE TRANSFIGURATION

Jesus took three of His disciples along for one of His personal devotional times. There He had a discussion with Moses and Elijah! The guys who went with Jesus were so out of their minds that they had no recollection of what Jesus and Moses and Elijah were discussing. They were simply too flabbergasted to say or think or do anything coherent. That is what a thorough encounter with God in prayer for breakthrough does—it wrecks you!

Jesus—clothes and all—became as bright as the whitest bright light (like looking into the sun, but greater). Moses and Elijah weren't scared off by this. They were used to it, they had seen Jesus like this before, in heaven.

The disciples were wrecked. Again, a normal prayer meeting for Jesus. Jesus went from glory to ever-increasing glory.

The supernatural should become normal for us. The Bible is full of visions, dreams, words from God, and supernatural encounters.

> After six days Jesus took with him Peter, James and John the brother of James, and led them up a high mountain by themselves. There he was transfigured before them. His face shone like the sun, and his clothes became as white as the light. Just then there appeared before them Moses and Elijah, talking with Jesus.

Peter said to Jesus, "Lord, it is good for us to be here. If you wish, I will put up three shelters—one for you, one for Moses and one for Elijah."

While he was still speaking, a bright cloud covered them, and a voice from the cloud said, "This is my Son, whom I love; with him I am well pleased. Listen to him!" (Matthew 17:1–5)

Did you notice that last line? Sonship. That identity was the key to Jesus's prayer life. It was the key to Jesus's authority. Jesus didn't go around questioning who He was. He knew who He was. Because of that, everyone else either thought He was crazy, demon-possessed, or someone who truly came from God. Why? He knew who He was. "I'm the Son, and my Father loves Me and is pleased with Me."

Think of the Christmas movie *Elf*. Buddy the Elf knows he's an elf. He not trying to prove it to anybody, he *is* an elf. Everyone thinks he's crazy, but that's just who he is. No one can even begin to understand him because they haven't seen what he's seen.

Jesus knows He's the Son of God. He spent eternities past in the presence of His Father, creating worlds by His own authority. He knows who He is.

Do you know who you are? Do you spend enough time in heavenly places, experiencing His glory, to *know* you are a son or a daughter of the King? Knowing who you are changes everything.

When you know you're a child of the King, it'll change the way you think. It'll change the way you perceive others around you. You'll begin to love them like He does. It'll change the way you speak and interact with people. And, it will change the way you pray. Oh yes! You're a son in union with Christ. Jesus knows what His Father's will is. He doesn't have to ask Him about it; rather, He enforces it!

God said, "This is My son." He wasn't talking to Jesus. Jesus very well knew His identity. He was telling the disciples. They needed to know the identity of the One they follow. He was foreshadowing what the disciples' and our relationships with God would be like: Father–son; Father–daughter.

God spoke three things about identity that we have to understand in order to be someone about whom God says, "Listen to Him!" (1) "This is My Son…" *I am a child of God. God is my Father.* (2) "…whom I love…" *God loves me.* (3) "…with Him I am well pleased." *God delights in me.*

Get God's identity for you deep in your spirit, and you'll start praying differently. You'll know God's will about a lot of things—healing, salvation, who to love with no strings attached (everyone), who to talk to about Jesus (everyone), and more.

"When the disciples heard this, they fell facedown to the ground, terrified. But Jesus came and touched them. 'Get up,' he said. 'Don't be afraid'" (Matt 17:6–7). People who don't fully know they're sons yet respond this way. They can only take so much.

"When they looked up, they saw no one except Jesus. As they were coming down the mountain, Jesus instructed them, 'Don't tell anyone what you have seen, until the Son of Man has been raised from the dead' (Matt 17:8–9). Jesus knows people can only handle so much. Jesus knows that people don't understand that He's been living in shimmering brightness like the sun. He gets it. But He revealed that glory to us. He wants us to seek it out. Seek Him out—His glory, His heaven, His face, His kingdom, His righteousness. Are you ready to seek Him out today?

3. GETHSEMANE

"Jesus went out as usual to the Mount of Olives, and his disciples followed him" (Luke 22:39). Do you see that? "*As usual…*" This was a normal prayer time for Jesus. This time he took three disciples with Him to stay close. This was His usual place for prayer. He went to the Mount of Olives—to a Garden called Gethsemane.

Do you want to pray like Jesus? There's a price to be paid in prayer.

> On reaching the place, he said to them, "Pray that you will not fall into temptation." He withdrew about a stone's throw beyond them, knelt down and prayed, "Father, if you are willing, take this cup from me; yet not my will, but yours be done." An angel from heaven appeared to him and strengthened him. (Luke 22:40–43)

103

As usual—a normal prayer time for Jesus. Why should we be surprised when an angel shows up at our prayer time? Now, we shouldn't brag about it, Jesus certainly didn't. But it shouldn't be so shocking in the body of Christ to have supernatural activity as a normal occurrence in prayer. Most people think, *Well that'd be cool,* but are you willing to pay the price? Here's the price:

> And being in anguish, he prayed more earnestly, and his sweat was like drops of blood falling to the ground. When he rose from prayer and went back to the disciples, he found them asleep, exhausted from sorrow. "Why are you sleeping?" he asked them. "Get up and pray so that you will not fall into temptation." (Luke 2:44-46)

Temptation? Temptation to what? Run away. Jesus was prophesying that what was about to happen next would be too great for them if they didn't paid the price in prayer like Him. That is key to praying like Jesus. The price is paid in prayer, beforehand. We can't shut down and go on a prayer vigil "strike" until we receive the answer. We can't go on a hunger-strike fast until Jesus answers. Don't even think about it. That is manipulation. Don't try to manipulate God.

The prayer must be stored up. We have to regularly get into God's space and experience the heavenly places that God has for

His sons and daughters, developing relationship with our Father. Then we're ready.

A LIFESTYLE OF PRAYER

Here's what we learn from Jesus' example:

- Jesus's prayer times were not mere religious exercise. They were spiritual experiences and breakthroughs.
- We were not meant to pray without breakthrough. Maybe you need to broaden what you are praying for. Tie your prayers to actions.
- Diversify your prayer portfolio in order to start seeing breakthrough. Maybe you're only praying for your needs; pray for others, etc. Maybe you pray for the nation; pray for the world. Maybe you pray for your family member's health; pray also for their finances.

Next, how did Jesus teach us to pray? "This, then, is how you should pray: 'Our Father in heaven, hallowed be your name, your kingdom come, your will be done on earth as it is in heaven'" (Matthew 6:9–10).

If you're thinking, *I don't know if it's God's will to heal,* question: Is there sickness in heaven? No, because God's will is done in heaven. God's will is that there would be no sickness. God's will is to heal. Period. And Jesus says, "Whoever does the will of my

Father in heaven is my brother and sister and mother" (Matt 12:50).

Jesus also taught us more about prayer in Matthew 6 and 7: (1) Don't pray to be seen. (2) Pray with an attitude of forgiveness. (3) Pray heaven to earth. (4) Seek the kingdom. (5) Seek righteousness (He has hidden things *for* you because there is joy in the search). (6) Ask God, because he gives. (7) Know God, or rather, be known by God

Jesus thanked God for the five loaves and two fishes. At the Lord's Supper, Jesus gave thanks. Afterward, they sang a song of praise to God. Thanksgiving is a weapon in prayer. I bet Jesus did a lot of thanking in His prayer time.

Praying in the Spirit is also a great weapon in prayer. Jesus didn't need this weapon, but we do. Pray in the Spirit loud and long. Thank Jesus loud and long. Seek His face. Seek His kingdom. Be seated with Him in heavenly places. Thanksgiving is one of the ways to be a good steward of God's blessing in our lives.

Before Lazarus's resurrection, Jesus offered up a weird prayer: "Father, I thank You that You have heard Me. I knew that You always hear Me, but I said this for the benefit of the people standing here, that they may believe that You sent Me" (John 11:41).

Have you ever thought about why Jesus prayed like that and how that is an example for us? I have. Here's a hint: He's a Son talking to his Dad. It sounds strange as a prayer to us, because we're used to churchy show-prayers rather than real conversations between a Father and child. But the supernatural reality of His world was more real to Him than our natural reality. He had spent eternities past with His Father in perfect harmony and unity, creating worlds and having conversations. It's an example of Jesus knowing His identity and authority as Son. Do you know your identity as a son or daughter of God?

Then, what did Jesus say after He prayed the Son prayer? "Lazarus, come out!" He commanded the dead man; He didn't command God the Father, or an angel, or the Holy Spirit. And He didn't beg or plead with God. Jesus KNOWS what God's will is. He commanded the dead man to come out.

Additionally, read Jesus's prayer in John 17. It takes up most of the chapter and is just as weird as the Lazarus prayer. He prays like a Son, an heir, someone who knows His Father's will and business.

HEALING PRAYER

When Jesus prayed for healing, His prayer pattern was simple. Jesus raised people's faith, and then He commanded the healing.[5]

Jesus commanded us to heal the sick—to do the works of the Father. "Heal the sick, raise the dead, cleanse those who have

---

[5] See Appendix C for a full listing of Jesus's healing commands.

leprosy, drive out demons. Freely you have received; freely give." (Matt 10:8).

Jesus said that people ought to believe on the basis of the miracles themselves (John 14:11), and then He said that whoever believes in Him would do even greater things than these in His name (John 14:12).

Jesus does not create us in a way that we are incapable of obeying His commands. "Well, I'm just an introvert." So what? So was Jesus, and it didn't stop Him. "I'm insular. I like to worship seated in introspection." If the Bible commands us to shout, I'm going to shout! If the Bible commands me to sing a new song, I'm going to sing to the Lord no matter my level of gifting. If the Bible says pray in the Holy Spirit, I'm going to do that. If the Bible says I should eagerly desire to prophesy, I'm going to get after it. These are commands. They're not suggestions. They're not offered with the disclaimer, "If you have the gift . . ." No. "Freely you have received; freely give."

Others of us have trouble with the command to "be holy." But if God says you can be holy, who are you to say you can't? Jesus said to go everywhere and heal. Heal who? Only the people you are led to pray for? No. "Heal the sick."

Prayer is meant to connect to breakthrough and spiritual experience. Prayer leads into the next action and risk in faith you will take.

If you're not experiencing breakthrough in prayer, you obviously don't have enough people to pray for. Diversify your portfolio. Start praying for people who are strangers. Start praying for people at Walmart, for waiters and waitresses (and tip them extravagantly), for people on social media (write them more than they bargained for). Just do it. "Freely you have received; freely give."

So, to beg God to heal someone means that you feel you have more compassion than God himself. Think about it: God has more compassion for that person's situation than we do. But when we beg Him, we assume He's not paying attention (which is not true Scripturally) or that He doesn't care (which is also not true Scripturally). That's why we never see Jesus begging God for healing. It's not how Jesus prayed.

We can err on the other side too. Don't command God to heal someone. That shows you don't understand and respect His authority over you. It's disrespectful. Who do we think we are?

Okay … Don't beg God … Don't command God … So what should we do?

Do what Jesus did. Do what the early church did. Command sickness to go, in the name of Jesus. *Oh, but that feels strange!* Do you want breakthrough or not? It takes steps of faith that feel strange. It wouldn't be called "faith" if it was fact already. It's faith because it's a risk in the Spirit.

Jesus taught us to speak to problems and invaders and tell them to go. "Say to this mountain . . ." (Matt 17:20, 21:20; Mk 11:23). "Say to this mulberry tree . . ." (Lk 17:6). Jesus spoke to the storm. He cursed the tree. He didn't command God or angels or curse the people who tended the tree. He spoke to bodies ("Be healed," "Be clean," "Get up"). Sometimes the commands He gave were instructional to people ("Stretch out your hand," "Take your mat"). This is why I will often ask people to test out their pain level to see what God has done.

In Matthew 17, the disciples couldn't cast out a demon. They asked why. Jesus said, "Say to this mountain . . ."

Matthew 13:58 does not say Jesus *tried* and *could* not heal in His hometown; it says He *did* not. Why? Lack of faith does not hinder God's ability. It shows an unwillingness on our part to steward His purposes on the earth well. In such a case, if Jesus gave us what we asked, it wouldn't be a true blessing for us, because it would add sorrow (Prov 10:22). We don't beg. We minister.

Praying like Jesus means we raise people's faith, command healing into their body, and expect/test for breakthrough.[6]

---

[6] For so much more Biblical basis for the supernatural work of God, see my Doctoral Dissertation, which bears the same title as this book, specifically "Chapter 2: BIBLICAL-THEOLOGICAL LITERATURE REVIEW" and "APPENDIX A: MAKING THE SUPERNATURAL NORMAL IN THE OLD TESTAMENT."
https://jaredstepp.files.wordpress.com/2019/05/making_the_supernatural_normal_jared_stepp_doctoral_project.pdf

DISCUSS/REFLECT

How are Jesus's prayers presently different than yours? Specifically, how can you pray more like Jesus today?

_____

_____

_____

_____

_____

_____

Have you ever commanded healing into someone's body? If so, how did they react? If not, how do you think they'd react? What's the worst that could happen?

_____

_____

_____

_____

_____

_____

_____

_____

_____

_____

_____

(Much worse happened to Jesus.)

111

STUDY

Read John 11 (Jesus Raises Lazarus). Ask Jesus to speak to you as you read.

What stirred in your spirit as you read? How did God speak to you?

_____

_____

_____

_____

_____

How did Jesus raise faith in the disciples, Martha, Mary, and everyone listening?

_____

_____

_____

_____

EXERCISE

Who are you praying for, for healing right now? Have you commanded their body to be well, sickness to go yet? Raise faith in them. Command their body to be well and then expect/test the results. Pray multiple times if you have to.

Chapter 12 –
What If Jesus Meant What He Said About Miracles?

Have you ever seen a relationship so broken that you knew it needed a miracle to be restored? Have you ever been a part of such a relationship?

We learned that a friend of ours was in an affair with a coworker. What followed was a string of prayer times and prophetic times, text message strings and phone calls.

What we didn't know was that the affair was simply the tip of the iceberg for the couple. The rift in their relationship ran deep into so many levels of sin, mistrust, disappointment, hurt, pain, and loss. And the pain for each ran deeper to horrible atrocities that had been done to them as children—lifestyles growing up where it seemed like God was absent. We listened and prayed, listened and encouraged, listened and spoke the Word of God and life. We got them to counseling and got them good books. They were broken. They didn't trust each other. Their deep-seated mistrust worked into every area of their lives.

I could go into gory details, but I promise it's not worth it. Just believe me when I tell you, whatever your craziest imaginations about what could have been possible in their relationship, it was probably that bad or worse.

Nevertheless, we had this intense, burning belief in our souls, and we kept declaring it to them at every step and every turn: *Nothing is impossible with God.*

But why did we believe that? How were we able to look them confidently in their eyes, staring down all their demons, and say, "Nothing is impossible with God"? Well, that's the most simple and complicated question of all because it needs more stories, but before we get there, let's dive into the Scripture.

MOUNTAIN-MOVING FAITH

In Matthew 17:20, Jesus had just finished casting out a demon from a little boy, after the disciples had failed at the same task. The disciples later asked him why they couldn't drive it out like He could. That's where we get to verse 20 . . .

> He replied, "Because you have so little faith. Truly I tell you, if you have faith as small as a mustard seed, you can say to this mountain, 'Move from here to there,' and it will

move. Nothing will be impossible for you." (Matt. 17:20) (Also see Matt. 21:21–22 and Luke 17:6)

Wait … what? Nothing is impossible *for God*, right? Sure, there are other Scriptures that say that, and we know that to be true. Even atheists admit that if there is a God, nothing would be impossible for Him. That's all good. But it's just not what Jesus said here. What did Jesus say? Nothing will be impossible *for you.*

What if we believed that nothing is impossible for us?

Some of you are thinking, *Yeah! I like that! Woot! Woot!* Others of you are cringing because we've all been trained in very humble and religious ways to give all glory to Jesus. Let me set you at ease: That is still true. We still give all glory to Jesus *and* we walk in the confidence that Jesus gave to us. How does Jesus receive glory if we ignore what He said and never step fully into the place of confidence in our authority that He gave us? What if we believed that nothing is impossible *for us*? What if we believed Jesus meant what He said about miracles?

Before we get back into what Jesus said about miracles, we're going to rewind into the Old Testament and look at one of God's names.

MIRACLES ARE IN GOD'S NAME

Psalm 77:14 says, "You are the God who performs miracles; you display your power among the peoples." Wait … Isn't this supposed to be about one of God's names? Where is it in that verse? Well, it's actually hidden in the Hebrew. It's something that gets lost in translation a bit. The phrase is literally like this: "You are the God, Worker of Miracles." This is one of His names. This is what distinguishes Him from all false gods. God's name is Worker of Miracles. It's central to His character and personality. The supernatural is normal to Him. We have two realms: natural and supernatural; God just has one. It's all the same to Him. He's always supernatural. When He shows up, miracles are normal.

Now, let's dive into the New Testament and see Jesus in His natural state.

JESUS IN HIS NATURAL STATE

He went down with them and stood on a level place. A large crowd of his disciples was there and a great number of people from all over Judea, from Jerusalem, and from the coastal region around Tyre and Sidon, who had come to hear him and to be healed of their diseases. Those troubled by impure spirits were cured, and the people all tried to touch him, because power was coming from him and healing them all. (Luke 6:17–19)

So here's Jesus in His natural state, and power is coming out from Him as people touched him. All kinds of diseases were healed for all kinds of people. Impure spirits were leaving. No one could escape from His power.

What if Jesus meant for each of us to move in the same miraculous power that He had? What if? So again, how were we able to look that couple confidently in their eyes and say, "Nothing is impossible. We believe you're going to thrive through this"?

EVIDENCE THAT GOD IS WITH US

Don't you believe that I am in the Father, and that the Father is in me? The words I say to you I do not speak on my own authority. Rather, it is the Father, living in me, who is doing his work. Believe me when I say that I am in the Father and the Father is in me; or at least believe on the evidence of the miracles themselves. Very truly I tell you, whoever believes in me will do the works I have been doing, and they will do even greater things than these, because I am going to the Father. And I will do whatever you ask in my name, so that the Father may be glorified in the Son. You may ask me for anything in my name, and I will do it. (John 14:10–14)

Miracles are evidence that God is living in us. Not evidence to *us*—evidence to *others*. We already know that God is living in us because of His constant work in our lives, but others can't see that work as easily. There must be tangible evidence of God's work in us.

Why doesn't the Bible primarily highlight Jesus going around and healing people's emotions? Or doing miracles of reconciling relationships? Or miracles of giving huge financial gifts to the poor? These are all great things, and they all happened in Jesus's ministry. But the primary focus in Scripture is on the miracles of physical bodies being healed. Why? I believe it's because those "foolish things" confound the wise. The weak things overpower the strong (1 Cor. 1:27). Physical miracles are visible and viable. They are evidence.

I have a confession to make: God loves me … *a lot*. I've been the victim of His overwhelming grace and mercy every day of my life. And I've been ruined by seeing God do many impossible, miraculous things that are tangible evidence to me (and to His world) that He is love and He is good. I've been ruined because I can never ever settle for just going in religious circles again. I am fully committed to seeing the raw, authentic power of God in my world. He's alive, and I'm fully convinced.

Now here's a secret … *Shhhh … It's just you, me, and everyone else* … God loves YOU a lot. *You've* been the victim of God's overwhelming grace and mercy in your life. And you can be in a church that is consistently seeing God's raw, authentic power at work in our world.

What if Jesus actually meant that we would do greater miracles than He did? What does that mean? Is it simply because there are more of us? It's just greater in amount? Yes, I believe it does. But it's bigger than that. Does it mean, that we will do greater quality of miracles, meaning miracles that are more consequential to our world? Yes, I believe it does. So greater in quantity, and in quality, which matches the context of "Ask whatever you wish in My name." It also matches the context of Jesus saying the reason for our greater works is His journey to the Father. When He's with the Father—risen and victorious over sin and death—then He's fighting for our purposes on the earth.

This is the Man who had just raised Lazarus from the dead (in John 11). What kinds of "greater miracles" are even possible? Paul would say, "beyond what you can ask or imagine." The Bible has recorded even wilder things, to be sure—parting of the sea, water from a rock, earth swallowing 10,000 people, fire burning a drenched sacrifice and all of the water around it on command, a donkey talking, and more. Don't limit your imagination.

So, here's the rub: We all think that it has to do with our faith, but it doesn't. Jesus had (and has) greater faith in us than we ever could have. We don't have to have faith in our faith. All we need is belief that Jesus Himself meant what He said. If Jesus meant what He said about us seeing greater miracles than He did, then it's a certainty. We are destined as sons and daughters in the kingdom to see greater miracles than Jesus saw.

JESUS SENDS OUT 72

After this the Lord appointed seventy-two others and sent them two by two ahead of him to every town and place where he was about to go. He told them, "The harvest is plentiful, but the workers are few. Ask the Lord of the harvest, therefore, to send out workers into his harvest field. (Luke 10:1–2)

This is for everyone. Jesus was about to send 72 people out to spread the kingdom through God's miraculous power. This was not a moment for the 12 apostles. Not only that, but Jesus was specifically asking for *more* workers. It's not like these 72 were supposed to be an exclusive group.

The more people who grasp the power of God, the greater the move of God. *We* are the move of God. Get off the bench, and get into the game. Begin to believe that Jesus meant what He said. Begin to believe for God's best—not because of *your* faith but because of *His*.

Jesus commissioned them, "Go! I am sending you out like lambs among wolves. Do not take a purse or bag or sandals; and do not greet anyone on the road" (Luke 10:3–4). This is so interesting. There was a reliance here on God's provision in this supernatural environment. This was a building up of their faith. This exercise of taking nothing for their journey was like a faith building trust fall in that Jesus was specifically directing them to trust His words and His faith. Jesus has faith for provision where we don't.

Jesus continued, "When you enter a house, first say, 'Peace to this house.' If someone who promotes peace is there, your peace will rest on them; if not, it will return to you" (Luke 10:5–6). In Matthew's version of this instruction, Jesus said, "If the home is deserving, let your peace rest on it; if it is not, let your peace return to you" (Matt. 10:13).

So what is that? How does this happen? You walk into a house, and, then, how is it that you let your peace out to rest on it? It has to do with the presence of God—His perfect peace resonating out of you.

Then how do you let your peace return to you? Evidently, if someone is rude to you and kicks you out of their house, there is the possibility that we could leave the house with less peace in our inner world than when we walked in. There is an active quality to getting into God's space of peace again. This is a skill that we need to exercise multiple times a day, every day, our whole lives. I know it's a slight rabbit trail from the subject of miracles, but it will change your life as you practice it. Let your peace return to you after every negative interaction in your life. Our soul is easily thrown from peace. We just have to be very practiced at getting it back.

What if we practiced letting our peace return to us every time we were thrown off a bit? We'd never be disconnected from God's miraculous power in our lives.

Stay there, eating and drinking whatever they give you, for the worker deserves his wages. Do not move around from house to house. "When you enter a town and are welcomed, eat what is offered to you. Heal the sick who are there and tell them, 'The kingdom of God has come near to you.' (Luke 10:7–9)

Then, in Matthew's version again, Jesus commanded, "Heal the sick, raise the dead, cleanse those who have leprosy, drive out demons. Freely you have received; freely give" (Matt. 10:8).

"But Pastor Jared, *Jesus* heals the sick!"

True, true—100% true. That's also not precisely what He said. He told *us* to do it. What if Jesus meant that He has given *us* authority to give His miracles and His kingdom away?

I believe the Bible. I believe it in its original context, to its original audience. Jesus told *them* to do it, and there's even more evidence for that.

Believers have the greatest miracle of salvation and Holy Spirit living inside us. What if we believed we could "freely give" miracles away? Here's more context for what Jesus is saying . . .

The seventy-two returned with joy and said, "Lord, even the demons submit to us in your name."

He replied, "I saw Satan fall like lightning from heaven. I have given you authority to trample on snakes and scorpions and to overcome all the power of the enemy; nothing will harm you. However, do not rejoice that the spirits submit to you, but rejoice that your names are written in heaven."

At that time Jesus, full of joy through the Holy Spirit, said, "I praise you, Father, Lord of heaven and earth, because you have hidden these things from the wise and learned, and revealed them to little children. Yes, Father, for this is what you were pleased to do. (Luke 10:17–21 NIV)

Did Jesus *really* mean that they shouldn't rejoice about exercising authority? Not likely. He was rejoicing with them. He was simply putting priority on the greatest miracle, which is the miracle of someone entering into the kingdom of heaven.

THE SPIRIT WITHOUT LIMIT

"For the one whom God has sent speaks the words of God, for God gives the Spirit without limit" (John 3:34). What if Jesus actually meant that God gives His Spirit without limit? What kinds of great things should we be believing for daily?

Most people believe that the Spirit of God comes and goes like in the Old Testament, but in John 14:16, Jesus said that His Spirit would be with us forever. The Old Testament way is done. The Spirit of God can come upon us without limit.

GOD'S FAITH FOR MIRACLES

Mark 11:22 can be rendered as, "'Hold on to God's faith,' Jesus answered." Now, I know your Bible probably doesn't say that. The original Greek says *"echete pistin theou,"* which is literally

"Hold onto the faith of God." Five of fifty-five translations I looked at got this verse right. The other translators are getting cute with it, but it's even clearer in the Aramaic. Bottom line: Jesus said and meant, "Hold onto God's faith," not the other way. It's God's faith that we're to hold onto here, not ours. God's faith is the faith for the miraculous. Our faith is the faith for salvation, but we don't have to strive for miracles; we just have to rest in God's faith. He has all the reservoir of faith we'll ever need.

> "Truly I tell you, if anyone says to this mountain, 'Go, throw yourself into the sea,' and does not doubt in their heart but believes that what they say will happen, it will be done for them. Therefore I tell you, whatever you ask for in prayer, believe that you have received it, and it will be yours. (Mark 11:23-24 NIV)

Speak to the mountain. "Well, pastor, I'm not really comfortable talking to an inanimate object." Ok, cool. Are you ok staying stuck behind it? Because that's where you'll stay until you start speaking the way Jesus taught you to speak. What if we believed Jesus's instruction to speak to our world and command it to look like heaven?

PRINCIPLES OF BELIEVING JESUS ABOUT MIRACLES . . .

Miraculous Necessity – We *need* miracles because they are part of God's nature. His natural state is miraculous because Jesus is alive. If we believe Jesus is alive, then we are obligated to prove it to our world. We can't do that without the miraculous. We *need* to make the supernatural normal.

Miraculous Motive –Jesus was motivated by compassion. Every time He was moved with compassion, He did something miraculous. I believe compassion is a key and a secret that will unlock our prayers. Compassion—not sympathy. Sympathy is helpless while compassion, Biblically, has to act. Our motive for miracles is compassion for the person in front of us.

Miraculous Engine – The miraculous engine is faith and our position to the Father, not specific words or actions. Sometimes there were no words or actions when Jesus healed people. Consider the woman who touched the edge of His cloak or the many others who pressed in to touch Him. Our Father and His Son are believing for us, and we come into awareness of that reality, agree with it, and align our purposes with His. Miracles will happen.

Miraculous Result – The real result is not just a healed body. It is belief, praise, forgiveness, repentance, and being fully convinced of Jesus. The purpose of miracles, drawn from Acts 1:8, is for our world to see that Jesus is alive. Not all people who see miracles are going to respond to them by receiving Jesus. Jesus didn't have 100% of the people He healed come to faith in Him. I've seen people not respond myself, but when they see God's power, they'll have to reconcile it in their minds. At worst, you'll give them something that bothers them. But much more often, they'll respond with faith and belief.

Miraculous Confession – Not all people we pray for get healed. We're not fully like Jesus yet. Nevertheless, more and more are being healed. The percentage is definitively going up. We refuse to make excuses for why people *don't* get healed. The Bible does not, so we won't either. We'll go to Jesus personally in our quiet time and ask Him, but we don't have to give excuses.

The way of our world is a trajectory toward death because of sin. The question is not "why do bad things happen?" Instead, it is "why would God step into time and space and change things for good?" Easy. Because He's good, and He's love.

Miraculous Clarity – *Always* believe for God's best. Where do you need a miracle? I hear too many people say to me, "Well, I'm good." Obviously, you don't understand what's at stake here. We *must* believe God for His best (in our finances, marriage, job, physical healing, family members who need Christ, houses to sell, boldness to talk about Jesus, etc.).

Maybe we need God to set up opportunities to help bring someone in your life to Jesus—family members, friends, neighbors, strangers. We need something that changes the paradigm in the conversation—something that shows them the reality of the authentic power of God.

Rather than the "hamster wheel" of pointless discussions that go in endless circles and on to soapboxes about religion (and then politics, past mistakes, randomness, and pointless small talk), consider: What is it that has the power to break that cycle? A miracle does. Why not believe God for His best? Why not bring heaven to earth?

What is happening in the person's life that they think is impossible? What's a deep desire or something wholesome they want most? Target it, and pray the prayer of faith with them.

So, I never told you what happened with the first couple— our friends whose relationship had every level of mess, sin, pain and mistrust.

Jesus broke through. I can't even tell you the extent of the amazing ways He did. He taught them to love again, trust again, live again, hope and dream again. There is not only restoration in their relationship, but each of them are thriving as individuals like they never thought possible, ministering to and lifting up others.

Be encouraged. Nothing is too hard for God!

DISCUSS/REFLECT

What do you believe would happen in your life if you fully believed what Jesus says about miracles? How can you take steps to change your thinking today?

_____

_____

_____

_____

_____

Why is God's faith for miracles better than your faith? How can you partner with God's faith for miracles in your life and for others?

_____

_____

_____

_____

_____

STUDY

Read back through the Scriptures listed in this chapter. Ask Jesus to speak to you as you read.

What stirred in your spirit as you read? How did God speak to you?

_____

_____

_____

_____

Read them again, and specifically, ask God to raise your faith as you read.

EXERCISE

Now that your faith is rising, pray for a miracle you prayed for previously, again. How are your prayers different this time? Now check the results.

Chapter 13

Love and Power

Love and power have a beautiful, holy alignment in the Scriptures. Every time Jesus is said to have had compassion on people, what did He do? He moved in power. He healed somebody. He realized that what was going on with them didn't look like heaven, so He changed it. The love (compassion) of Jesus motivated Him to move in power.

In John 3:16, God the Father's love produced the most miraculous event the world had ever seen: God became human. Love and power—they are inseparable twins in the kingdom of God. If we are to look like God, then we had better start pairing love and power. Love without God's power is impotent and useless. Power without God's love is reckless and hurtful. They balance each other with gorgeous kingdom parity.

If we're to look more like God today, then we need both love and power. This is not an "either/or" kind of thing. This is not a "well that's *your* gifting" kind of thing. This is a *kingdom* kind of thing. If we're in the kingdom and we're going to spread the kingdom, then we are the agents of God's love and power. Again, love and power are inseparable twins in the kingdom.

TYING LOVE WITH POWER

> . . . so that Christ may dwell in your hearts through faith. And I pray that you, being rooted and established in love, may have power, together with all the Lord's holy people, to grasp how wide and long and high and deep is the love of Christ. (Ephesians 3:17–18)

We need God's power to even adequately grasp His love!

Paul wrote to young Timothy about his power gifting. Scripture isn't clear what the gift was, but it is obvious that it was a power gifting.

> For this reason I remind you to fan into flame the gift of God, which is in you through the laying on of my hands. For the Spirit God gave us does not make us timid, but gives us power, love and a sound mind. So do not be ashamed of the testimony about our Lord or of me his prisoner. Rather, join with me in suffering for the gospel, by the power of God. (2 Timothy 1:6–8)

This talk with Timothy was about power. Paul wrote about a power gift that was imparted to Timothy through the laying on of hands and prayer. Then he included love and a sound mind. Power and love must go together, and we arrive there with a transformed mind.

Additionally, Paul wrote to the Corinthian church about spiritual gifts in chapter 12 of his first letter, offering them a proper foundation for them. He followed that up with chapter 13—the most famous and powerful treatise on love. Then he went right back into discussing the powerful manifestations of Holy Spirit in chapter 14. This was not an accident. The chapter markings weren't there in the original letter. In fact, 1 Corinthians 12–14 is one complete section of Scripture, and it's all about the power manifestations of Holy Spirit, operating in love.

The love chapter was never meant to be taken out of that context. Naturally, I do think the love chapter is quite useful in many other contexts as well. However, let's see it how Paul, through inspiration, intended it—how his original readers read it. In Paul's mind, the most excellent "way of love" is tied inextricably to demonstrations of God's power. Love has no voice without the power of God.

LOVE AND POWER GO TO CHURCH

First Corinthians 14:1 says, "Follow the way of love and eagerly desire gifts of the Spirit, especially prophecy." This is the passage that ties it all together: "Follow the way of love *and* eagerly desire spirituals," or spiritual manifestations. The word "gifts" is interpolated in there by the translators. It's really "spirituals" *pneumatikos*, which means Holy Spirit *here*, Holy Spirit *there*, bits of Holy Spirit *everywhere*. Holy Spirit is showing Himself, manifesting, coming out of the unknown into the known. That's what *pneumatikos* means from 1 Corinthians 12:1 and 14:1. That's what we're talking about. Holy Spirit shows the world that God is real—that God is *here*. Holy Spirit shows up and shows off, doing what only He can do, pointing people to Jesus.

Here we see more of the marriage between the way of love and the power of Holy Spirit. The two cannot be separated in the kingdom. Paul wrote, "For anyone who speaks in a tongue does not speak to people but to God. Indeed, no one understands them; they utter mysteries by the Spirit" (1 Cor. 14:2).

I don't know about you, but I want to utter mysteries in the Spirit. It's a free gift for every believer—to utter mysteries in the Spirit. When we don't know how to pray, He prays. Awesome! But tongues are to be used with wisdom and not in a place with a bunch of people have no clue what's going on. That sounds loving.

Paul continued, "But the one who prophesies speaks to people for their strengthening, encouraging and comfort" (1 Cor. 14:3). Here we see the New Testament purpose of prophecy. It is for strengthening, encouraging (or exhorting), and comfort. The waters are deep on this subject, and we'll explore more later. But for now, recognize this: The purpose of prophecy is tied to love.

Strengthening someone else—that's what love does. Encouraging others—love does that. Comforting people—love again.

Now, we as Christians are called to eagerly desire to love people through speaking with the power of God's specific words for them. It says we should "eagerly desire" to prophesy! Prophecy is speaking God's specific words to someone else. When we wrap it in love, it comes out as strengthening, encouragement, and comfort.

"But God often shows me dark stuff." Yup, me too. But how do we love with what He has shown us? Love says that when I see the dark, I need to point the person toward the prophetic opposite of that thing. What is the gold that needs to be called out in order to crush the darkness? We're invited to think in prophetic opposites. The waters are *really* deep here. But just to give you a taste: If I'm praying for someone and I see depression, I begin to call out, "He is the glory and the lifter of heads; He is the changer of countenances." That's one of God's names, and it is the prophetic opposite of depression. God will show you dark stuff sometimes (me too). Welcome to Holy Spirit's mentoring program. Now, seek Him for how to beat it.

> Anyone who speaks in a tongue edifies themselves, but the one who prophesies edifies the church. I would like every one of you to speak in tongues, but I would rather have you prophesy. The one who prophesies is greater than the one who speaks in tongues, unless someone interprets,

so that the church may be edified. Now, brothers and
sisters, if I come to you and speak in tongues, what good
will I be to you, unless I bring you some revelation or
knowledge or prophecy or word of instruction? . . . If then
I do not grasp the meaning of what someone is saying, I am
a foreigner to the speaker, and the speaker is a foreigner to
me. So it is with you. Since you are eager for manifestations
of the Spirit, try to excel in those that build up the church.
(1 Cor 14:4–6, 11–12)

Firstly, from these verses, there are some manifestations that
build up more than others. Paul specifically identifies prophecy as
one of them. Prophecy is amazing. It is built to call out God's gold
in people—to see them the way God sees them. Prophecy lets us
look past whatever mess may be true about them and opens our
understanding to see the future possibilities and the specific picture
of who God is shaping them to become. It's awesome, and it's
something that is useful in any context—anywhere with anyone.

Word of knowledge is another. It's supernatural knowledge
that God gives you about someone else. Healing is another one.
It's useful anywhere and everywhere.

Prophecy, word of knowledge, and healing are the specific
power tools that will help us at work, at a restaurant, at Walmart,
or with our neighbors. These gifts will empower us to see people
come to Christ. All the other gifts interact with those three in
helpful ways. But those are the ones that need to surface. And if

we lean into them more, we'll see greater results in ministry and Christian witness. These three are the most visible demonstrations of God's power in Jesus's life and ministry, and we will focus on them in the next section of this book.

Secondly, Holy Spirit's manifestations are sometimes exercised in weird ways that do not follow the way of love, according to Paul. The best place to demonstrate signs is with unbelievers, but we have to know which ones will convey love to them the most—healing, word of knowledge, and prophecy rank at the top of the list. The other manifestations are trickier to use in loving lost people—not *impossible*, but trickier.

THE WAY OF LOVE

Love says "see a doctor." Follow your doctor's advice—not blindly, of course. Be wise. But follow your doctor's advice. Love also says I cannot be offended regarding miracles. That means I can't be offended at God if I don't get what I'm asking for immediately. Regarding healing, love says I can't be offended at God, even if someone doesn't get healed at all. Regarding people, love says I can't be offended at people when they think they've experienced a healing but then haven't. I can't be offended at God if the sickness or pain comes back later. This is all the way of love.

Love also is willing to look silly in order to get someone free, whether that be simply getting out of your comfort zone, God asking you to do something that looks silly, or praying for someone multiple times because the healing wasn't completed the first time.

This is how love relates to power (the law of love; the way of love). Love says "I will stop praying for someone, no matter how much power I am sensing, if I recognize they will not feel loved if I continue." Where's the line? How do you know when to pray for someone? Who to pray for? When to stop praying? The answer to all of those questions is "follow the way of love" as you're moving in power.

Take those you're praying for as far as they're able to go—as long as the love-meter is still ticking. As soon as the love-meter is about to run out, that's when it's time to stop. Personally, I've never felt specific leading from the Lord to go beyond that.

Without power, people might care that *you* love them, but they won't care that *Jesus* loves them. They'll blame that love on you, and then you'll have to fulfill unrealistic expectations of love toward them your whole life. You'll never meet human expectations in your own power. Our love is built to connect people to His love. God's love is shown practically when He does things that only He can do.

In fact, you can yell at your world, "I LOVE YOU!" all you want. They'll just yell back, "NO ONE CARES!" In fact, so much of the church has been trying this for years, and that's precisely the response they get. That's why you *need* the power of God! *We* need the power of God!

After Peter was endued with love from Jesus, what was the first thing he did? Feed the sheep? Nope. That's not what he did. He waited for power. Why? Because without the power of God, we literally have nothing to feed the sheep with. Peter was endued with love first and given a calling from Jesus to do something impossible—to do something that love, in and of itself, cannot accomplish. So, he waited until the power came at Pentecost.

Many times, that's what Holy Spirit does with us too, that's part of how He mentors. He wraps us in His love because that's essential. Then He calls us to change our world, inspiring us to go seek the supernatural tools with which to do so.

Billy Graham's ministry (now through his son, Franklin) has touched countless lives. I love what they're trying to do there in bringing people to Jesus. They report a 6% retention rate after 1 year and 2% after 2 years.[7] I understand, as I've been a part of the follow up teams for those things. You call people the day after, you send them things, you call them again and again. At best, half of the people might ever communicate with you. But hey, 2% of those people do stick, which is still good for the kingdom.

Contrast that with the Argentinian revival—probably the greatest revival of our generation. Millions of people gave their lives to Christ. It was filled with outrageous power manifestations from Holy Spirit and miracles. 15 years later there is 80% retention rate.[8] Not even close. The retention with the outrageous revivals

---

[7] McIntyre, Patrick. *The Graham Formula*. Page 12. Mammoth Springs, AR: White Harvest, 2005.

[8] Tennant, Carolyn. "Catch the Wind of the Spirit." Lecture. Evangel University, Springfield, MO.October 2017.

that happened in America at Azusa Street, Brownsville and Toronto? 80%.[9]

Those are just cold facts. And the Scripture echoes this. We *must* move in power. We can't expect to change our world *for* God without undeniable encounters *with* God. That is the tool set that leads to transformation.

The fruit of the Spirit grants permission. In other words, if we don't have love, joy, peace, and the rest (Gal. 5:22–23), we don't get permission to represent Jesus in power. Meanwhile, the powerful manifestations of the Spirit are the authenticity tools. They'll *know* we are Christians by our love, but they'll *verify* that *they* need to be Christians as His power works through us. And, statistically, they'll remain Christians when we get enough of both the love and power of God in them that they can't ever turn back. That's a supernatural work too—the sanctifying work of Holy Spirit whereby we become new creations.

If you've experienced the love of God and you know that God has called you to do great things for Him, it's time to grow in both love and power. By the way, the Great Commission makes it clear that He has called you to do great things for Him: Make disciples of *all* nations. Since we've been baptized in His love, we've heard His calling.

---

[9] Tennant, Carolyn. "Catch the Wind of the Spirit." Lecture. Evangel University, Springfield, MO.October 2017.

How many of us right now are walking in the fullness of what God has called us to accomplish for Him? Obviously, we're not (as the "big-C" Church, collectively), or else the whole world might be saved by now.

All of us could be walking in our callings more. So, where's the disconnect? I would submit that it's primarily a power outage. A lot of parts of the church talk about power, but far fewer are doing God's works. The power of God for church leaders is a, "put up or shut up" topic (1 Cor 4:19). Then there are other parts of the church that are operating in power but stink at the love side.

We have to do both. I refuse to compromise on either end of this. It's too important. We can be a church that has power encounters everywhere we go, bathed in love.

DISCUSS/REFLECT

Have you ever prayed for or witnessed to someone too long, after your love-meter has run out? Have you not pushed far enough, when God was still active? What happened?

_____

_____

_____

_____

_____

_____

Have you ever tried to love someone to Jesus and they didn't care? How could you interact differently with them in the future?

___

STUDY

Read 1 Corinthians 14. What stirred in your spirit as you read? How did God speak to you?

___

How can people run out from God's love in church? Do you think it's easier to jump start a church into power, or direct a moving ship like Paul does here? (Moving ship – 100%) The power must be present first for this discussion to matter. How can you immerse yourself in power?

___

EXERCISE

Practice praying for someone until the love meter runs out. Say things like, "are you still ok? We can stop anytime. God's love for you is so huge!" You might be surprised as to how long it takes.

Section 4:

Gateways to the Supernatural

All of the gifts of the Spirit are amazing and profitable, and we want all of them. They all have a perfect place in the body of Christ. However, there are certain gifts of the Spirit that Jesus and the apostles used on a regular basis *outside* of church meetings. These gifts are palatable for anyone. Excuse my reference, but I call these three gifts the "gateway drugs" to the supernatural. In other words, these are the kinds of supernatural things that are gentle enough in their approach that they won't freak people out. What hopefully *will* freak people out is that they just experienced the power and love of the living God. The prayer worked, and their life is now changed for the better. That's how Jesus did it. The "gateway drugs" to the supernatural that will get people hooked are prophecy, words of knowledge, and healing.

Chapter 14:
Prophecy Foundations

The church must demystify prophecy. Roughly 35% of the Bible is prophecy. Paul commanded us to eagerly desire to prophesy (1 Cor 14:1). Prophecy is not fortune-telling; it is sharing God's desires and words. Prophecy is not on the same level as Scripture. Instead, prophecy is judged against Scripture.

I remember a relationship with another person in my life that, to be quite vulnerable, had annoyed me. The person had come to me for prayer and advice over the course of many years, but I never knew how to break through for her. She struggled with anxiety and depression because of speech problems and a mental disorder. The conversations troubled me because they were the same every time—same problems, same feeling like I had given her nothing to break the cycle. Then, God gave me a new lens to see her through, and for the first time, I saw into her soul.

In that prayer time, she was especially anxious, depressed, and repeating herself continually in almost an angry way. But I saw her for the princess she was, and I saw something in her that needed to be called out. So, I turned on the faucet of prophetic encouragement and poured out encouragement until everyone was red in the face, embarrassed with the praise that was gushing out of me.

My wife and I watched her countenance literally change to joy. Every time I saw her from then on, she was lit up with God's joy. She was becoming the prophetic gold that had been called out in her. She was a joy to be around. It changed her *and* me—a watershed moment for me in calling out the prophetic gold. There are brand new countenances—permanent changes for good on the other side of prophetic moments of breakthrough. We *need* this.

Simply put, prophecy is giving away God's words for a specific time, place, and person/people. As a further analogy, prophecy is putting our finger on God's pulse—hearing His heartbeat for people, hearing His voice, calling out God's gold in them.

You can hear God's voice. There are at least twenty-seven ways of listening to God's voice.[10] In fact, if you're a believer you *must* hear God's voice (John 10:27). Therefore, prophecy should be a normal part of the Christian life. Discerning whether you're

---

[10] See Appendix B for the full listing, with Scriptural examples.

hearing God's voice is where people get stuck. Most believers don't have a hearing problem; they have a discernment problem.

DISCERNING GOD'S VOICE

How do you know when your thoughts, impressions, pictures, and so on are God's voice? The following filters will help you discern.

1) Does it line up with God's written Word, the Bible? Most Christians exaggerate their knowledge of the Bible. This requires study most of the time. Go ahead and internet search that phrase that you think you might remember. Stop *assuming* you know, and *actually* know the Bible. Without a grounding in the Word of God, your prophetic journey will either stall or get heretical. Dive deep into the Word of God. This is the first and most important filter through which to run your words and pictures from God. If it does not line up with the Word of God, it's not from God. *Full stop.* Don't move on to filter two. Seek another word or picture from God.

2) Does it line up with God's character? This is more subjective than number 1 (although it's still based on the Bible), but it is necessary to think this way to start exercising your discernment muscles. If the word or picture you're receiving reeks of accusation, that is probably coming from you or from the enemy (the accuser). Then it's time to seek another word or picture from God. Don't move on to filter three. But if it feels and smells like something God would say, you can move on to filter three, four or five.

3) Ask someone who you know hears from God. First Corinthians 14:29 describes an environment where prophets are speaking and others are helping them discern. There were schools of prophets in the Old Testament and groups of prophets in the New Testament. The wisdom and discernment of others in the body of Christ can help you discern your word more clearly.

4) Does it confirm what God has already been speaking to you? If it doesn't, you can't necessarily rule it out; simply don't hold it as tightly. Often, God will speak to us in multiple groups of words/pictures that confirm each other.

5) Does it come true? Do parts of it that can come true quickly happen? Sometimes you need to write it down and just wait to see if it comes true later. Sometimes there is responsibility in walking out a prophetic word as well, but there needs to be a path for this. Also, be aware that the fulfillment can sometimes be in the distant future. However, every prophecy will have action steps right now (even when the step is "wait"), or else why would God have shared it now?

ASK "WHO?" AND "WHEN?"

The first questions I generally ask the Lord about a word/picture I'm receiving is "who?" and "when?" Who is this Word for, and when am I supposed to share it?

Many times we run into confusion when we share what we have heard from God with the wrong person or group and/or at the wrong time. Ask these questions continually, and you will develop the habit of discerning the answers in ways that are clarifying.

THINK IN MARCHING ORDERS

In the military, a marching order is only good until there are new marching orders. What would happen if we received a word from God in an area, and then God wanted to change His order? What if the time and season had changed, but we were still stuck on the other orders because we were so sure of that word from God? People do this often. The point is to hear from God continually so that we know when His marching orders change.

Unlike the written Word of God, the prophetic is specifically designed to give us temporary orders. God is allowed to change His mind on these things as He guides us. He does not change His mind about what is written in the Bible—that is why He gave it to us in such concrete form. Therefore, if a prophetic word from God is a re-articulation of a Biblical principle, then that is the only time it is timeless and not merely a marching order. Otherwise, we need to think about the words, impressions and visions that God has given us in terms of marching orders. They absolutely are from God. They are binding. Obedience is required. However, they are not eternal. God will give us new marching orders, sometimes more often than others.

THINK IN TRAJECTORIES

A prophetic trajectory is when God shows us the direction of a certain expression of His kingdom in our life or in others. Many times, God will give us a picture of what that expression of the kingdom will be like in the future. A vision of a house without strife or a church that is life-giving, etc. We often fail to realize that time is VERY fluid in the prophetic. The trajectory that is being set by God is moving us toward that picture in the Spirit. That means obedience to that prophetic leading is movement along the trajectory toward that picture. Anything that is moving toward God's picture is being a good steward of God's Word. Things that do not move us in that direction are poor stewardship.

DEALING WITH BAD NEWS IN YOUR SPIRIT

We don't have to hear from God very long before we start discerning bad news about people or circumstances. Prophecy's purpose is "encouragement, exhortation, and comfort" (1 Cor. 14:3). In other words, if people are not being encouraged, exhorted or comforted when we tell them what God is saying, then we're doing it wrong. Holy Spirit is our Comforter, and He works entirely in the realm of love. Therefore, He will pull against our tendency to share news with someone that does not work in harmony with love and comfort.

That should create a holy tension in us to carefully choose our words, tone, heart and timing when sharing the prophetic. That is Holy Spirit's way of mentoring us to make sure that our words only build others up (Eph. 4:29). We have to lean into His heart on this and be willing to constantly improve under His direction. Holy Spirit is an amazing teacher.

As mentioned in our previous chapter, when we hear bad news, we should begin to think in prophetic opposites that will inform our intercession and our interactions with people. For example (this is not an exhaustive list) …

God shows us...	Pray and speak...
Depression	Crowned with glory (Ps 3:3)
Broken & hurting	Wholeness of heart
Harsh	Patient lovingkindness
Unforgiveness	Love for people – no enemies
Religiously rigid	Richly gracious
Frenetic energy	Powerfully peace-filled
Dormant anger	Bubble-ready joy

THINK IN MOSAIC

"We know in part and we prophecy in part" (1 Cor 13:9). Many times, we see only pieces of the mosaic of God's communication and not the entire picture. That can be humbling to realize. Again, God is drawing us deeper into His heart. The point of all of this is intimacy: personal relationship with Jesus. If we feel like we're hearing from God but we're not growing deeper into an intimate relationship with Him, we're doing it wrong.

The reason God will share things "in part" with us is so that we seek Him out for the rest. It's like He's saying, "Here's a present, and I've wrapped it up in a mind-blowing aspect of my character that you need to take the time search out." Each piece of the mosaic is a clue to the whole of that picture, and that little mosaic is part of an infinite mosaic that makes up the personality and ways of our God. Have fun searching Him out for the next pieces. Listen for those pieces to sometimes come through others. Enjoy the ride with Him through His personality and ways. Holy Spirit is funnier than we think.

Of the (at least) twenty-seven different ways that God speaks in the Scripture, God will engage many of them in any mini-mystery that we are seeking out. Begin to see each piece of the mosaic and the empty spaces and arrange them with Holy Spirit's help. When we step back from the pictures, we will always see Jesus (Rev 19:10). I promise this journey into His heart will be pure pleasure.

DISCUSS/REFLECT

Reflect on your experience with prophecy to this point. How have you seen things go right and wrong? Focus more on what went right.

_____

_____

_____

_____

_____

What has kept you from listening for God's voice for others more? How can you remove some of those obstacles in the next season?

_____

_____

_____

_____

_____

STUDY

Read Acts 21:4, 8-14 (Agabus's prophecy to Paul). What stirred in your spirit as you read? How did God speak to you?

_____

_____

_____

_____

Did Agabus miss it? Did Paul miss it? How was the reception of the prophetic word affected by discernment? Why did the action Paul took differ from what others thought he should take?

_____

_____

_____

_____

_____

_____

EXERCISE

Ask for a word from God for someone right now. Run it through the filters of discernment. Ask God "who?" and "when?" Don't assume that you know this. Write it down and be obedient to what God shared.

_____

_____

_____

_____

_____

_____

_____

_____

_____

Chapter 15 –

Follow the Breadcrumbs

Prophetic revelations don't come out of nowhere. Spend time with God. Practice hearing from God. Take risks of faith so that you KNOW in these moments that it's Him.

First Samuel 9 describes a nation-changing moment, and the prophet Samuel had to be ready:

> "About this time tomorrow I will send you a man from the land of Benjamin. Anoint him ruler over my people Israel; he will deliver them from the hand of the Philistines. I have looked on my people, for their cry has reached me." When Samuel caught sight of Saul, the LORD said to him, "This is the man I spoke to you about; he will govern my people." (1 Sam. 9:16–17)

Samuel was listening to God, and the Word from God to Him was that He would have to listen *more* tomorrow!

God is working in breadcrumbs. We long to see the big picture, and once we do, we often stink at doing something productive with the big picture information. So, God knows that many times we need little bits of information at a time. It helps us grow and keep listening.

Following the breadcrumbs is an old movie trope. Wile E. Coyote used a trail of breadcrumbs (birdseed) to lure Road Runner out. Detectives like Sherlock Holmes, Dick Tracy, and Batman would follow every little detail until they solved the mystery. We also have a trail to follow.

God told Samuel, "You're going to meet Israel's first king tomorrow." But what if Samuel quit listening and picked the wrong guy? Bad news, right? For sure. Or what if he quit listening and missed the moment?

God works in breadcrumbs. This is one of His ways—the manner in which He typically does things. He gives us what we need to know to make decisions in that moment, and then He gives us the next piece, and then the next piece. God works this way so we can keep tuned into His voice and make adjustments on the fly. Think about a time where God has done that for you.

Saul approached Samuel in the gateway and asked, "Would you please tell me where the seer's house is?"

"I am the seer," Samuel replied. "Go up ahead of me to the high place, for today you are to eat with me, and in the morning I will send you on your way and will tell you all that is in your heart. As for the donkeys you lost three days ago, do not worry about them; they have been found. And to whom is all the desire of Israel turned, if not to you and your whole family line?" (1 Sam. 9:18–20)

Look at this; this is so fun! Samuel worked in breadcrumbs. He looked a lot like God here. He led Saul with the next piece, and the next piece *only*. Today you'll eat with me, tomorrow's going to be great.

"I'll tell you what's in your heart." Why did this have to wait until tomorrow? I don't think Samuel knew yet! Samuel spoke only what he knew and stalled in order to seek God about this man and find out what else is in his heart.

Next, Samuel quelled Saul's fear about the lost donkeys with a word of knowledge. Then he pours out gold onto Saul: "You and your whole family line are the objects of Israel's desire. Breadcrumbs.

Saul answered, "But am I not a Benjamite, from the smallest tribe of Israel, and is not my clan the least of all the clans of the tribe of Benjamin? Why do you say such a thing to me?" (1 Sam. 9:21)

We sometimes want to respond this way to words from God. "I stink at life"—false humility, self-loathing remarks, all the reasons why not. But here's the truth: People who give correct words from God have learned the art of receiving words from God. It involves discernment. When we hear from God, sometimes we get the initial impression correct, but then we discern incorrectly how to express it to someone else. Sometimes it's a matter of who to express it to or when to express it. Sometimes we still need to catch the attitude and heart in which to express it. So, if someone gives us an incorrect word from God, it's generally a matter of failed discernment.

For example, suppose I'm sitting here, and I feel like God has given me a word about someone being brokenhearted. I might immediately interpret it as the person who's closest to me. That may be right or wrong. I need to ask God about that.

So, God says, "No, it's about this other person."

"Okay, Lord." Then your immediate thought is to go to them right away. But what if God has better timing? So, you ask Him.

He stalls.

What now? In my experience, God often stalls because He wants to speak to you about the heart of your approach. In other words, how are you going to love the person to victory? Is it going to be by saying, "Hey, God told me you're brokenhearted"? No way. So how will it happen? Ask God about that. When you have clarity, proceed. That's discernment. It's huge.

There are a number of opportunities for us to slightly miss, but there's generally a correct impression from God buried in there. Look for that and receive it, because people who give correct words from God have learned the art of receiving words from God.

SEEK UNDERSTANDING

Saul ends with a great question: "Why do you say such a thing?" In other words, if there's a word from God we don't understand, it is always appropriate to seek understanding from Him.

Why do you say such a thing? That's a good question. That's a question that is worth asking God almost every time He speaks to you, whether that be to you directly or through someone else.

When Saul asks this, Samuel could have turned to God in his spirit at this moment and said, "He's right! Why him? This guy's kind of a bum." Samuel didn't turn to Saul and say, "You're going to abuse your power, rebel against God, go stark raving mad, take your army after a shepherd boy, consult a witch, and then kill yourself on the battlefield." Even though Samuel could have said that and might have known that in the spirit, he didn't say that because he was intent on calling out gold.

RELATIONSHIP MATTERS

Over the next few verses, Samuel takes time with Saul to get to know him and build rapport. That's important for a word from

God to be received. Build rapport. Take time with the person. Maybe Samuel was even seeking clarity from God about Saul or how to present the Word to Saul in a way that it would be received.

> As they were going down to the edge of the town, Samuel said to Saul, "Tell the servant to go on ahead of us"—and the servant did so—"but you stay here for a while, so that I may give you a message from God." Then Samuel took a flask of olive oil and poured it on Saul's head and kissed him, saying, "Has not the LORD anointed you ruler over his inheritance?" (1 Sam 9:27–10:1)

Samuel gave Saul a bunch of prophetic knowledge. "This is what is going to happen next …" He gave Saul three things that would soon happen. In verse 5 is the most important . . .

> "After that you will go to Gibeah of God, where there is a Philistine outpost. As you approach the town, you will meet a procession of prophets coming down from the high place with lyres, timbrels, pipes and harps being played before them, and they will be prophesying. (1 Sam. 10:5)

These guys will be accompanied by music. There's something about music that helps connect us with the moving of God's Spirit.

PROPHESY TOWARD TRANSFORMATION

> The Spirit of the LORD will come powerfully upon you, and you will prophesy with them; and you will be changed into a different person. Once these signs are fulfilled, do whatever your hand finds to do, for God is with you. (1 Sam. 10:6–7)

I believe Samuel had an idea of what kind of person Saul was in his heart. This is why he called out gold and prophesied necessary transformation. Notice the words, "You will be changed into a different person." Also, notice what Samuel didn't say. He didn't say, "You're super paranoid and rebellious in your heart, and you're actually quite a foolish person and a terrible leader." He stuck with calling out the gold. He went right to the transformation part: "This is who you need to become in order to win—in order to be a good king."

Find the gold. Call out the gold.

> "Go down ahead of me to Gilgal. I will surely come down to you to sacrifice burnt offerings and fellowship offerings, but you must wait seven days until I come to you and tell you what you are to do." As Saul turned to leave Samuel, God changed Saul's heart, and all these signs were fulfilled that day. (1 Sam. 10:8–9)

Wait … The heart change wasn't supposed to happen, according to Samuel's prophecy, until *after* Saul met the company of prophets. Did Samuel get it wrong? Look back. What did Samuel say in verse 6? "You will be a different person." This is more than the change of heart mentioned in verse 9.

Saul needed a change of heart in order to take the steps of obedience to become a different person. Breadcrumbs. God gives one step at a time. Saul had to have a change of heart even to trust God's Word through Samuel enough to obey what God said to do. If Saul didn't obey, there would be no different person coming at all. That's how the prophetic works—how God's words work.

PROPHECY IS FOR EVERYONE

When he and his servant arrived at Gibeah, a procession of prophets met him; the Spirit of God came powerfully upon him, and he joined in their prophesying. When all those who had formerly known him saw him prophesying with the prophets, they asked each other, "What is this that has happened to the son of Kish? Is Saul also among the prophets?" A man who lived there answered, "And who is their father?" So it became a saying: "Is Saul also among the prophets?" (1 Sam. 10:10-12 NIV)

Do you see the absurdity of this scene? It was so wild to everyone that it becomes a saying in Israel! As if, "I've seen it all! Saul's a prophet now!" In other words, Saul was not the prophet type, not the spiritual type, not really even a good guy. Yet he prophesied. That's weird.

"Who is their father?" was a status dig at these prophets. In other words, these prophets are leaderless, fatherless nobodies. Saul is a somebody; we know his daddy. Saul was rich—he had servants and a posse—but here he was, slumming it with these prophets. This wasn't a compliment, but it beautifully speaks to the fact that prophesying is for everyone—from the nobodies to the future king. If you're a believer, the playing field gets leveled. We all receive the right, the privilege, and the command to prophesy. "Eagerly desire spiritual gifts, especially to prophecy" (1 Cor. 14:1).

WHAT'S THE NEXT STEP?

Let me tell you another story. Imagine you're in Germany in 1949, directly after WWII. Hitler, the monster, is dead. The National Socialist party is dead. But there's another little boy who walks into church one day. A brooding 9-year-old little boy, doing poorly in school and rebelling against his parents.

But his mom received a word from God for him about the sin he had just committed but not admitted. The word broke through. Then she spoke to him about Jesus. The power of Jesus fell in his life. He committed himself to be a Jesus follower, sought God, and was baptized in the Holy Spirit as a 10-year-old in 1950.

Many years later, that little German boy saw over 76 million decisions for Christ through his life and ministry. His name is Reinhard Bonnke, and he started an evangelistic ministry called

Christ for all Nations, which has ministered all over the world, especially in Africa.[11]

Follow God's breadcrumbs.

DISCUSS/REFLECT

Write down a couple times in your life when you've had to follow God's breadcrumbs. Were you ever frustrated? Confused?

_____

_____

_____

_____

Has God ever called you deeper into His heart while showing you only one piece at a time? Did you recognize that is what He was doing at the time?

_____

_____

_____

_____

_____

_____

_____

_____

[11] Bonnke, Reinhard. *Living a Life of Fire: An Autobiography*. (E-R Productions LLC, 2010).

STUDY

Read 1 Samuel 10:13–27 (The rest of Saul's crowning story).

What stirred in your spirit as you read? How did God speak to you?

_____

_____

_____

_____

_____

_____

Assess how Saul, Samuel, and others (Saul's uncle, etc.) stewarded the prophetic word. Was Samuel faithful? What about Saul?

_____

_____

_____

_____

_____

_____

_____

EXERCISE

Ask for a word/picture from God for yourself right now. Does the word build on other things that God is doing in your life? How does it shape and add texture to what God has already done in you?

Chapter 16 –

Gold Diggers

Gold ore just looks like dirt—nothing special to look at. You might have some on the bottom of your shoe. It's worth as much as dirt in that state, until the refining process. It takes 14 tons of gold ore to get 1 bar of gold! It's all about the process. Processing gold involves pouring water over it—tons and tons of gushing water. When you bring out the gold ore, all you see is dirt until you gaze at it for a while. Then the flecks begin to show up.

I believe there is buried treasure hidden in each human. I have already teased this concept throughout the book. Now it's time to unpack it. It's time to learn to gaze at the dirt long enough that you see the flecks for your family, friends, co-workers, and even the people in your life who you haven't yet learned to love . . . or appreciate . . . or even like.

Yeah, there's gold in them too.

THE REFINER

The Bible talks about "gold refined in the fire" a few times, and it's not just about trials; it's about the perfection and beauty of what God has placed inside of us. Troubles sometimes speed that process up, but I believe that God wants to perfect us and call out gold in us through processes that are glorious as well—not just the trials.

In other words, when you're in trouble and mess and fire, there's purpose. The purpose is that God will still use trial to accelerate your growth. However, when you're not in trial, (1) your growth won't be stunted and (2) don't think that God is going to bring another trial just to perfect you. That's fatalism, and it's not the Bible's viewpoint. God is not the author of all the trials in your life, but He will help you beat them. God is refining you right now.

BURIED TREASURE

Psalm 12:6 says, "And the words of the LORD are flawless, like silver purified in a crucible, like gold refined seven times." God's words are what created us. God's words are inside of us. And the gold that's inside us continually flows from God's words spoken over us.

Paul unpacked God's treasure in us in 2 Corinthians 3 and 4:

And we all, who with unveiled faces contemplate the Lord's glory, are being transformed into his image with ever-increasing glory, which comes from the Lord, who is the Spirit. (2 Corinthians 3:18)

For God, who said, "Let light shine out of darkness," made his light shine in our hearts to give us the light of the knowledge of God's glory displayed in the face of Christ. 7 But we have this treasure in earthen vessels to show that this all-surpassing power is from God and not from us. (2 Corinthians 4:6)

Paul established a series of truths in 2 Corinthians 3 and 4:

- God created us.
- God is illuminating truth in our hearts.
- There's buried treasure in us.
- The bringing to light of that treasure will help us to look more like Jesus.

Let's build this out from the Bible a bit more.

Proverbs 25:11 says, "A word aptly spoken is like apples of gold in settings of silver." The words we speak can illuminate and even produce gold in others.

2 Timothy 1:14 says, "Guard the good deposit that was entrusted to you—guard it with the help of the Holy Spirit who lives in us." There's a good deposit in us. Those are mining words.

Holy Spirit is in us, and He's a treasure. He wants us to let Him out more and more to affect our world.

John the Baptist was called the greatest prophet by Jesus (Matt 11; Luke 7). He was not the greatest predictor of future events, but he had the greatest message. He saw the gold in Jesus and called it out. He saw the gold in the Israelites and called it out. He saw the gold for future Christians—baptism in the Holy Spirit—and called it out.

John was seeing the treasure by hearing God's voice, and He was the first one to recognize Jesus clearly for who He really was. Buried treasure needs called out. The key is that we have to be constantly looking. Gazing. Gaining God's perspective, God's lens, God's view, God's eyes for people. God might highlight people for you. You will simply be drawn to them and won't know why at first. Then God will show you how to see them and call out good things.

You have a responsibility to gaze at your family long enough to call out these good things in them—to see them like God sees them. Your world is skilled at calling out the worst in them, so you must learn to call out God's best. It is a necessity for thriving and even surviving spiritually.

PROPHETIC CONFIRMATION

One of the primary purposes of calling out the gold prophetically in people is confirmation. Jesus already knew who He was; John the Baptist was simply confirming. In the case of

Gideon, it was not confirmation—he didn't see what God saw. The man was hiding and basically rebuked an angel for telling him he was a mighty man of valor! Gideon only began to see after some convincing and refining—some "gushing" over him of God's words, offered through the angel.

In King Josiah's revival (2 Chronicles 34–35), the whole community had gold called out for them. They found the Bible, the book of the Law, which they had lost. They read it, renewed covenant, and began worshipping God again. When God shined light on the gold they possessed as a community, they responded. They became what God had designed them to be. Powerful.

Then there was Barnabas. His birth name was Joseph, but he was renamed Barnabas or "Son of encouragement." It was an earned name. Barnabas mentored Saul and brought him into the church. He spent much of 13 years with him, saw him transformed into "Paul," the powerful, miracle-working apostle who wrote a third of the New Testament.

How many times do you think the "son of encouragement" Barnabas called out the extreme insular thinker Paul and told him who he really is in God? He spoke gold into his life. It was while ministering alongside Barnabas that Saul's name was changed in the text to Paul. Barnabas was a supernatural encourager, full of the Holy Spirit and power. Barnabas went on an encouragement tour across the known world, speaking life and truth into all the churches.

GUSHING WATER

I believe we all have more noble thoughts than we are ever able to declare. The more you declare, the more they come, like an open faucet—like the tons of water gushing on the gold ore. If we never open the faucet, we get stuck on less noble thoughts about others. Encouragement that turns supernatural is like opening a faucet and speaking truth until the water gets hot.

So, what's a good starting place for your prophetic encouragement tour? Identity in Christ: We are royalty—sons and daughters of the King—and we reign as kings and queens in God's kingdom. Refer to Romans 6, Ephesians 2, and 2 Peter 1 (among other Scriptures).

God has placed treasure inside each human being—gold that cannot spoil, tarnish, or fade—creative genius from a good Heavenly Father who uniquely designed for you to recognize your royalty so that you can give away eternity.

See the gold in yourself. In order to have something to give away, we have to receive it first and daily from our Father. Some of us need to break ground in our souls and let God begin new construction with the raw materials He has placed there. Here's a tip for prophetic encouragement (calling out the gold): Turn weakness into strength. "You see that this was true about you, but here's the truth of what God sees in you . . ."

I'm not an encourager by trade. I'm a listener by trade—a listener to God and others. However, encouragement is the entry point to pour out God's design to someone. The prayer for people becomes, "God, give me eyes to see and ears to hear the rhythm of another person's soul as You see and hear it."

Then there's the turn—the change in tone when you've turned the faucet of encouragement on and it gets hot. Your human encouragement suddenly becomes a transformational word from God. You don't know how long the faucet will have to run before it turns hot.

One of the greatest examples of this for me is an extroverted evangelist friend of mine. She will talk to you passionately about anything. She was talking to me one time and began to encourage me. Then the conversation turned. Her the tone changed. She began to speak into my soul—into my future—with clarity about my passions and motivations. She presented a vivid picture of a better me, which hadn't been true yet but which I knew was God's destiny for me. She uncovered and called out gold in my life. It was a watershed moment for me—a turning point for good.

Today is a watershed. I am declaring a watershed moment for anyone reading this who is willing. Are you willing to call out gold in others? Are you willing to turn on the faucet of encouragement and let God take over? Are you willing to see people how God see them?

It's not like this is optional. Jesus did it all the time, and we are called to be like Him—sons and daughters who bear His name. Start with trying to see people differently—not as objects of pity but as magnificent, purpose-filled, and glorious. Ask God how He sees them. Once you see His picture, the words for it are automatic and easy.

If you've ever thought, "Lord, help me to love the unlovable," here's the truth: *No one is unlovable.* Holy Spirit knows exactly how to love everyone, and He's inside us. He is able to teach us exactly how to see the prophetic gold in every person around us.

Start with simple encouragement. Turn on the faucet. It generally takes a while for the water to get warm when you turn it on.

If you've ever been in an encouragement/prophetic prayer circle, where someone gets put in a "hot seat" and everyone encourages them, it always goes longer and longer. Why? Because you're turning on the faucet, and when God starts to take over and the water gets hot, it's hard to turn it off.

DISCUSS/REFLECT

Think about the times God has refined the dirt in you or someone around you into gold. If you can't recall one quickly, think about what it would be like if He did.

_____

_____

_____

_____

_____

How does simple encouragement turn into prophetic breakthrough? Have you ever "turned on the faucet" of encouragement and started to let it flow? What did it feel like?

_____

_____

_____

_____

_____

STUDY

Read Judges 6:11-7:14 (Gideon).

What stirred in your spirit as you read? How did God speak to you?

_____

_____

_____

_____

Have you ever felt like Gideon at the beginning of the story? How many others in your life probably feel something like him? How did the angel and then God produce gold in him?

_____

_____

_____

_____

_____

EXERCISE

Start writing a note of encouragement right now to someone you know well. Ask Holy Spirit to direct what you write. Then write whatever trite nonsense comes into your head until Holy Spirit takes over and it gets "hot" with prophetic encouragement. Take a moment to read over the note and discern. Refine the message if needed. Then give the person the note.

Chapter 17

Word of Knowledge Foundations

I can remember the exact place where I was standing—noises all around, people milling around. I had the opportunity to pray for someone for random things. I couldn't keep praying though. I was stopping and stuttering, and I didn't know what was happening. The Spirit of Christ inside me was trying to get my attention. And when I finally gave it to Him, He said, "He's got lower back pain." Boom: word of knowledge.

So I stopped and asked the man, "Do you have lower back pain?"

He answered, "Yes, for the past twelve or so years, I've been messed up in my back, man."

Jesus is so good. Do you see how good He is? The man was up here praying for something else, and Jesus said, "Yes, we'll deal with that too; but *while we're at it*—if it's ok with you—we're going to heal the twelve years of back pain you've been dealing with, because I love you, and I think you're amazing."

Jesus healed Him, *and* dealt with what was in his heart. And Jesus only addressed the heart issue *after* the back pain was healed.

A word of knowledge is supernatural knowledge from God that only He could know, which you can use to glorify Jesus. This is like a secret weapon to kickstart so many of the other gifts into action.

Many times a word of knowledge is the first thing that happens in a supernatural environment. The Bible says things like, "Jesus knew their thoughts …" The prophet Elisha was so locked into the knowledge from God that he knew all the movements of the Syrian king against Israel, "knowing the secrets he whispered in his bed chamber" (2 Kings 6:12).[12]

KICKSTARTING FAITH

I was talking to a lady and felt like God showed me she had headaches regularly, and she did, so we prayed. You better believe faith rose! And, afterward, I was able to say, "Jesus told me that because He loves you and thinks you're amazing, He's longing for

---

[12] There is a full listing of the biblical uses of words of knowledge in my Doctoral dissertation, which can be accessed for free here: https://jaredstepp.files.wordpress.com/2019/05/making_the_supernatural_n ormal_jared_stepp_doctoral_project.pdf.

relationship with you." You know she's going to notice when her headaches go away.

Seeking a word of knowledge is simple: *God, what do you want me to know about this person that will point them to Jesus?*

In my opinion, word of knowledge is the key secret weapon in making the supernatural normal. If you tap into this, it opens the door for everything else—healing, prophecy, miracles, faith, etc.

We receive supernatural knowledge from God more often than we think. We simply have to be ready to recognize and use it when it comes. God might speak through a sensation on your body. He might speak through your eye continually being drawn back to something on a person. It may be an inner sense of simply knowing, "Your daughter really loves school, doesn't she." God likely wants to affirm that and speak prophetically through you into her daughter's destiny.

God can speak words of knowledge ahead of time. You're praying for someone, and you hear something specific and strange. Write it down, and then be ready to give it away. Ask God "who?" and "when?" (just like with prophecy).

Word of knowledge is like a video game cheat code that accelerates progress in ministry. You can tell someone God loves them, or you can show them that, say, God knows their address— proof that God knows the details of their life and loves them.

Prepping for Healing

> But some of the scribes were sitting there, and reasoning in their hearts, "How is this person speaking like this? Blasphemy! Who has power to forgive sins except the only God?"
>
> And immediately Jesus knew in His spirit that they were thinking these things, and he said to them, "Why are you thinking these things in your hearts?" (Mark 2:6–8, JST).

Have you ever said to your kids, or another driver, or a friend (in your head), "What were you thinking!?" It's normally not a good thing, but look at this: God knows what you're thinking, and He still loves you.

Mark, the author, went to great lengths to make sure that his readers knew that these guys gave no physical indications about their opinions. They were "sitting there" and "reasoning"—not out loud but "in their hearts" (Mark 2:6). Mark, the narrator, shows that Jesus "immediately" knew "in His spirit" that they were "thinking these things" (Mark 2:7). Jesus even stated that their thoughts happened "in their hearts" (Mark 2:8). Mark wanted his readers to know that Jesus received special, supernatural insight from God in this moment. Jesus did not have time to perceive and ascertain with human insight that kind of knowledge. He immediately knew because of a word of knowledge from God.

This kind of knowledge is available to believers. What if the Holy Spirit is trying to get your attention with this kind of knowledge all the time? What if, instead of thinking, *Why's that person being such a jerk?*, a random thought floats through your head: *They were abused*? what if that's God speaking to you? And what if He's telling you that so that you can be a source of healing for that person?

"Hey, how are you doing today, really?" That question is so fun. It throws people off. "Jesus loves you."

Some of you need to care more. Your compassion-meter needs to dial up. Jesus was ready to heal the man, but he had to take care of his heart first.

THE APPROACH TO WORD OF KNOWLEDGE

> The woman said to him, "Sir, give me this water so that I won't get thirsty and have to keep coming here to draw water."
>
> He told her, "Go, call your husband and come back."
>
> "I have no husband," she replied.
>
> Jesus said to her, "You are right when you say you have no husband. The fact is, you have had five husbands, and the man you now have is not your husband. What you have just said is quite true."
>
> "Sir," the woman said, "I can see that you are a prophet. Our ancestors worshiped on this mountain, but you Jews claim that the place where we must worship is in Jerusalem." (John 4:15–19)

Notice Jesus's approach here. They're just chatting. Then, boom—Jesus moves in the supernatural. It's obvious to the woman. But He's done it in a way that is normal, and He furthers the conversation. That's the power of a word of knowledge. It was a simple fact but was completely mind-blowing to the woman.

Word of knowledge is simple, and it's one of the primary ways that Jesus moved in the supernatural during His life on earth. It validates spiritual authority—or at the very least spikes curiosity! The conversation will keep moving after a correct word of knowledge. Suddenly, the woman was after Him to teach her.

THE MAESTRO OF THE STORY (THE LAST SUPPER)

On the first day of the Festival of Unleavened Bread, when it was customary to sacrifice the Passover lamb, Jesus' disciples asked him, "Where do you want us to go and make preparations for you to eat the Passover?"

So he sent two of his disciples, telling them, "Go into the city, and a man carrying a jar of water will meet you. Follow him. Say to the owner of the house he enters, 'The Teacher asks: Where is my guest room, where I may eat the Passover with my disciples?' He will show you a large room upstairs, furnished and ready. Make preparations for us there."

The disciples left, went into the city and found things just as Jesus had told them. So they prepared the Passover. (Mark 14:12–16)

I have to ask you right now: What do you believe about Jesus? Jesus just gave the disciples a vision-level word of knowledge. If any detail was wrong, the whole thing would fall apart. Jesus just became the maestro in His story. The maestro—you know, the guy who has the authority and directs and tells the rest of the story how it's going to go.

Are there times when Jesus stopped just listening to the sounds of His world and started directing them? Oh yeah. Lots of them. Before the Triumphal Entry, He gave them a similar direct word of knowledge. What about when He calmed the sea? He pulled the authority card, but only within the parameters of the same rules in which we can pull the authority card and begin directing the music of our story.

What are the conditions in which we can become the maestros of our own stories? I don't have the market cornered on this, but I've seen God do enough crazy awesome things to observe a few things:

- 100% of the time, the supernatural doesn't work if we don't remember it and agree with it.

- The supernatural does work when the conditions are right to give God maximum glory. God will not share His glory with anyone else.

- Jesus is the author and completer of the supernatural. Well, duh—but sometimes we're not locked into that.

- It doesn't help to get weird. The supernatural is normal,
  and it works in normal, everyday environments. Jesus was
  just sitting by a well. The disciples just wanted to know
  what room to get for the Passover. It's about the person
  in front of us.

The key with words of knowledge is risk—boldness and
being willing to ask. With words of knowledge, you will have
immediate feedback. You're either right or wrong. Therefore, you
can refine your hearing at a much more rapid pace than with
prophecy.

THE BEST, EASIEST, MOST COMMON, AND MOST FUN . . .

It's the best when someone who you know is on the brink of
faith, and you just received a dramatic word of knowledge for
them.

Also, very commonly, you will feel drawn to someone. This
will happen literally everyday if you let it. The more you ask for
words of knowledge, the more you're going to be drawn toward
everyone.

It's the most fun when they get visibly affected by the word
(whether emotionally or receiving healing), because then you can
ask God what the spiritual significance is. "Jesus did this because
He loves you and is longing for relationship with you . . ."

THE SECRETS OF OUR HEART

"You want to be a coach, don't you?" I said.

"I want to be a what?" She replied, incredulous.

"You want to coach volleyball and basketball, don't you?"

"Yeah, but I never told anyone," She answered.

"God knows your heart, and He knows that you're not playing right now because of things out of your control. But you're going to play again, and He has plans for you as a coach. He loves that you want to be a coach, and He's going to use you."

The words had just started to roll out of my heart by that point, as they pierced the heart of this teenager who had been through so much. She had people reject, abuse, and tell her what she couldn't do her whole life. So even when someone came along to encourage her, she didn't believe them. But not this time. God shined light onto the secrets of her heart through supernatural knowledge (a word of knowledge), and everything in her heart became free game again.

When God reveals the secrets of the heart, the heart will open like a flower to Him and to people. Paul wrote about this to the church in Corinth.

> "But if an unbeliever or an inquirer comes in while everyone is prophesying, they are convicted of all and convinced of all, as the secrets of their hearts are laid bare. So they will fall down and worship God, exclaiming, 'God is really among you!'" (1 Cor. 14:24–25)

That girl walked into an environment where God's words were being poured out and the gold in her was being called out. This time, she couldn't convince herself out of the encouragement, and she couldn't run from God's love. She decided to become an all-in Jesus follower!

Truth:

1. The secrets of *your* heart are laid bare before our Father, and He still likes you. Does your heart need to open up today?
2. The secrets of others' hearts are available to you through Holy Spirit when we partner with Him for kingdom purposes, with His love in our hearts.

Who will you target for God's love?

NO MORE CONVINCING

She had been my neighbor for 6 years. We had a great relationship. My wife and I had invited her to church to watch our kids in their programs or for a special event probably 25 times. She was always interested but never came.

One day, God started speaking to me about her daughter, the things that happened to her, and the nature of their estrangement. So, I told my neighbor this information and asked her if I could pray.

Eagerly, she said yes.

In the prayer, out of nowhere, I declared that the love relationship with her daughter "will be restored *today*."

My neighbor bounced out to me the next day, freaking out. Her daughter sent her a text message that night: "I love you, mom." It was the first communication in fifteen years!

All of a sudden, I didn't have to convince her of anything. She was asking me, "What do I need to do to get right with Jesus?"

Supernatural knowledge makes human wisdom secondary. It puts courage and poise on the back burner. It says to our powers of persuasion, "Simmer down, now! You don't have anything useful to contribute here."

Too many believers are stuck in a rut of convincing people. In fact, it's so ineffective, they've given up. Jesus didn't do a lot of convincing. You were either in or out. You either saw what He did and believed, or you saw what He did and explained it away. But Jesus didn't beg or debate. He ended debates with supernatural knowledge, healing, and (sometimes weird) prophetic words (hello, John 6). Jesus often ended debate by using a word of knowledge.

THE BIG PICTURE

Further defined, words of knowledge are past or present realities/information that God uses to confirm His nature and pave the way for the good work He wants to do next.

A primary way to grow in hearing God's voice is to test if you're hearing God's voice. That comes through testing words of knowledge. If the knowledge is correct, you might be hearing right.

Follow that more. For many of you, this is the way you need to grow right now.

Categories of words of knowledge:
- God might give you a family detail
- Personal detail
- A picture of them doing something
- A time frame when something happened
- An illness or pain they're dealing with

How they come?
- A foreign thought
- A physical sensation
- A knowing
- A picture of them
- Writing
- Emotional sensation

DISCUSS/REFLECT

Have you ever been talking to someone and suddenly a rogue piece of information drops into your head about them? Did you think it was from God? How can you recognize more quickly when God is giving you a Word of Knowledge?

_____

_____

_____

_____

_____

_____

_____

_____

How often do you ask God for supernatural knowledge? What are some specific environments where you can ask God for knowledge this week?

_____

_____

_____

_____

_____

_____

STUDY

Read Mark 2:1-12 (Jesus heals the paralyzed man).

What stirred in your spirit as you read? How did God speak to you?

_____

_____

_____

_____

_____

_____

How does Jesus use a word of knowledge in the story? (Hint: verses 5 and 8–9.) How does this protect the paralyzed man's heart and spirit?

_____

_____

_____

_____

_____

_____

EXERCISE

Ask God to show you different people in your life about whom He wants to share knowledge with you. Ask God for specific emotional and spiritual breakthroughs right now.

Chapter 18

How to Know the Secrets of the Bedroom

(It's PG, I promise!)

"How to know the secrets of the bedroom"? Shouldn't it be how to know the secrets of the *heart*, Pastor Jared? Sure, but that's not actually what the Scripture says. It says "the secrets in the King's bedroom." That sounds super crazy, but it's all going to make sense in a minute. I promise, it's PG; but it's also going to be so fun.

In 2 Kings 6, we see something that's only possible because of the ridiculous, undeniable power of the living God. Hold on to your seat.

> Now the king of Aram was at war with Israel. After conferring with his officers, he said, "I will set up my camp in such and such a place." The man of God sent word to

the king of Israel: "Beware of passing that place, because the Arameans are going down there." (2 Kings 6:8–9)

These are words of knowledge—supernaturally God-given knowledge that would be impossible to know otherwise. This happened to Elisha over and over again.

This kind of knowledge is always purposeful. It's not a party trick. You'll see the purpose at the end of the story. Connecting to God's purpose for the supernatural is one of the keys to seeing God work in your life in this way.

So the king of Israel checked on the place indicated by the man of God. Time and again Elisha warned the king, so that he was on his guard in such places. (2 Kings 6:10)

Where you go will determine who you're with. If you don't want to be with jokers, don't go to places where jokers hang out. Position yourself so that you *have* to do the right thing. Joram, the foolish king of Israel, suddenly looked like a genius because he took advice from Elisha, the man of God.

He didn't just *hear* the advice; he took it in and acted on it. When you take advice from God (and men and women of God), God looks good! Even fools look wise when they listen to God.

The King of Israel had not increased his IQ even a bit—we'll see that later in the story—but he was leading well and making God look good by listening and obeying Him.

This enraged the king of Aram. He summoned his officers and demanded of them, "Tell me! Which of us is on the side of the king of Israel?" (2 Kings 6:11)

A little bit of justifiable paranoia here. What's happening for the Israelites shouldn't be possible. And it's kind of comedic for us who are reading the story.

"None of us, my lord the king, "said one of his officers, "but Elisha, the prophet who is in Israel, tells the king of Israel the very words you speak in your bedroom." (2 Kings 6:12)

There it is—the secrets of the bedroom. The man of God knows the secrets in the bedroom! Ok, ok. For real: the man of God knows anything and everything that he's willing to listen to God about. That means you can know anything God wants to disclose that you're willing to listen to Him about fully.

SECRETS OF THE HEART

God knows the secrets of the heart. Psalms 44:21 says, "Would not God have discovered it, since he knows the secrets of the heart?" The revealing of the secrets of the heart is specifically tied to prophecy in the Scripture. First Corinthians 14:24–25 says, "But if all are prophesying and some unbeliever or uninformed person comes in, he is convicted by all and is judged by all. The secrets of his heart will be revealed, and as a result he will fall facedown and worship God, proclaiming, 'God is really among you'" (CSB).

Here are some secrets about the secrets of the heart and God's knowledge of them:

1. They're safe with Him. The Secrets of your heart are safe with God. Why?

2. God will only reveal them to people who can help you. If it seems your secrets were revealed to someone who can't help you, then that was just intuition or a lucky guess— not God. God reveals real secrets to people who know His heart and act in accordance with His heart.

3. If you want to know the secrets of the heart, then you have to be willing to shepherd those people's hearts well. It sounds really fun to the know the secrets of people's hearts, but there's a cost. There's a responsibility. You have to love those people's hearts. Aim to heal the hurts and stoke the dreams.

God knows everything about you and will only use that information to build you up. Therefore, align your heart with God's so that you can be someone who knows everything about someone and will only use that info to build them up. Becoming a person who's ready to hear the secrets of the heart means that you will need to be faithful with that information and able to only build people up.

The secrets of the heart include:

- Deep wounds
- Deep regrets
- Wins and skills that we're not proud of
- People we don't know how we'd live without
- Dreams, goals, and plans that you secretly believe you can accomplish, but you're pretty sure others won't understand
- Secret sin
- Secret love
- Secret plans
- etc.

Who would you share those things with? There's a reason they're secret. Sometimes they're even secret from you. Sometimes you don't even realize some of the secret plans and motivations you have until God reveals them. But God knows everything about you and will only use that information to build you up.

Reimagine your life with all your secrets confronted. God knows your secrets, and He's the first person you should share those things with—both the good and the bad. He will *NOT* use them to hurt you. And if He reveals them to someone else—like they say, "I feel like God showed me . . . "—then He reveals them only to bring healing, hope, direction, or strength. God will help you deal with your secrets in redemptive ways.

What if you didn't have to shove away parts of your past that hinder you but could look the whole world in the eye, in spite of what happened? What if you weren't ashamed of that dream you have to start a business? What if you were confident that God can bring the right spouse, if you do your part (brush your teeth)? What if your emotional hurt from your childhood was such a beautiful scar that you could show it to someone going through the same thing and bring them healing? God wants that for you.

Next, reimagine your life as someone worth sharing secrets with. If you were to realize about your co-worker that they are suffering from depression, what would be your response? Like truly, what would you do? Not *altruistically* what do you *think* you *should* do, but what *would* you do? Would you wish you hadn't learned that information because you don't know what to do? Would you pray for them quietly, on your own? That's a good start.

Would you merely feel pity for them? Truly search your heart. All of us have done this, but it's not helpful. Pity will only teach you to treat them poorly. God won't reveal a secret to someone who's best response is pity. So, reimagine your life as someone worth sharing secrets with.

Would you find a way to encourage them? Would you check on them again? Would you ask to pray with them?

By the way, none of those things require that you reveal to the person what you know. It can be helpful to reveal it at times, but many times you have to reach out to help in the healing process before such an explanation of your revelation would be helpful at all.

OPEN OUR EYES, LORD

Let's read again about the king of Aram at war with Israel:

> "Go, find out where he is," the king ordered, "so I can send men and capture him." The report came back: "He is in Dothan." Then he sent horses and chariots and a strong force there. They went by night and surrounded the city.
>
> When the servant of the man of God got up and went out early the next morning, an army with horses and chariots had surrounded the city. "Oh no, my lord! What shall we do?" the servant asked.
>
> "Don't be afraid," the prophet answered. "Those who are with us are more than those who are with them." (2 Kings 6:13–16)

Fear is an enemy of clear vision and discernment in the Spirit. When you dwell in a fearful place, it will cloud your judgment from seeing a God who is enthroned in perfect peace. When you see your situation through the lens of fear, that fear will create certain outcomes for you. Lean into God and see things more like He sees them. That's when faith rises and fear melts.

> And Elisha prayed, "Open his eyes, LORD, so that he may see." Then the LORD opened the servant's eyes, and he looked and saw the hills full of horses and chariots of fire all around Elisha. (2 Kings 6:17)

The opening of eyes is a constant theme throughout the Scripture. It's a biblical term for discernment—seeing clearly in the spiritual realm. From the people who were in the wilderness, who could "see but never perceive, hear but never understand" in Psalms; to Jesus declaring the opposite of that Scripture to His disciples in John 12:40; to Paul declaring the opening eyes of the Gentiles in Acts 26:18; and his praying for the eyes of the heart to be enlightened for all believers in Ephesians 1:18 to know the power and love of God; and so many more Scriptures on this topic—God is in the eye-opening business.

This sort of scene happened with the two disciples on the road to Emmaus who did not recognize Jesus who had risen from the dead, and then again with Paul on the road to Damascus where he was physically blinded as a sign of his spiritual blindness; then he let Jesus into his life, and the man of God prayed, and he could see again.

There's physical blindness, which we're going to see in the next couple of verses, and then there's not seeing into the spiritual realm, which is what had happened for Elisha's servant.

As believers, you and I can see clearer and clearer into the spiritual realm. It's called discernment. Pray that prayer with Elisha and with Paul in Ephesians: "Open my eyes Lord." Or better yet, "Eyes, be opened!"

This is a prayer for spiritual discernment. This is one of the ways that the Holy Spirit manifests Himself in our world, and it's one of the most underrated and awesome ways in which the Holy Spirit works through believers. This is another secret to knowing the secrets of the heart: pray for discernment. "God, open my eyes."

Sometimes that prayer will give you more than you bargained for. It sometimes gives you access to problems that you will feel helpless against—and you are. That's why you must be completely plugged into the Holy Spirit. If He's inside you, He's capable of handling anything, and He will, through you—when you're ready.

When God tells me that someone was abused as a child, I'm immediately out of my league. I'm not a counselor, and I was not physically abused as a child. Immediately, I want to refer them to counselors, and I will. But most often, God has work for *me* to do first—that's why He showed it to me.

And so I send up a flare: "*HELP!!* Holy Spirit, where do I even start!?" And most of the time He gives me two things: (1) Love them (just to re-center me on the gold standard) and then

(2) He gives me a crazy picture in my heart. I'm like, *Why do I see a chihuahua right now?* "Just say it," "Uhhh, I feel like God showed me a chihuahua, does that mean anything to you?"

"Yeah," their eyes widen, "I had a chihuahua as a kid. It was the one sane thing in my insane growing up."

Alright, God, let's do this.

So, pray for discernment. "God open my eyes."

KNOW THE SECRETS OF GOD'S HEART

As the enemy came down toward him, Elisha prayed to the LORD, "Strike this army with blindness." So he struck them with blindness, as Elisha had asked. (2 Kings 6:18)

A reasonable request might have been, "God, please kill them all." They had come to kill *him* after all. But that's not what Elisha asked, and that's not a prayer that God wants to answer. Elisha knew God's heart and asked in accordance with that. I'm sure he was thinking, along with the Holy Spirit, *Let's have some fun with this!*

This request not to kill these men but to teach them a lesson is why Elisha is a guy God will share secrets with. Know God's heart, and He'll give you His secrets. This contrasts strongly with someone else in the story you'll see in a minute.

> Elisha told them, "This is not the road and this is not the city. Follow me, and I will lead you to the man you are looking for." And he led them to Samaria. (2 Kings 6:19)

Nice. Elisha's the only real Jedi. "This is not the road; this is not the man you are looking for."

Now look, I'm having fun with this, but supernatural knowledge from God is not a trick (although it *is* fun). It's not magic. There aren't rules to it that you can master—it's not "the force." It's you, developing relationship with the Creator God who loves you and who knows what's best for you. It's only out of that place that supernatural knowledge from God is useful.

The angels are like, "Ooh! This is fun! We each get to blind one of these dudes and walk with them to Samaria. *Hehehe* . . . I wonder if they'll know we're here!"

Elisha prayed to God, and the angels got to have some fun. Sometimes you have to pray to God, to give the angels permission to have some fun. They want to help. They want to have fun. Prayer opens the door for God to enable that.

> After they entered the city, Elisha said, "LORD, open the eyes of these men so they can see." Then the LORD opened their eyes and they looked, and there they were, inside Samaria. When the king of Israel saw them, he asked Elisha, "Shall I kill them, my father? Shall I kill them?" (2 Kings 6:20–21)

This is why God didn't share secrets with King Joram. King Joram was so excited. Do you see that in the text? He's basically clapping and jumping giddily, [scary voice] "Shall I kill them, my father? Shall I kill them? I do like a good execution. It calms my nerves. *Muahahahaha.*" Woah, woah buddy—settle down! King Joram doesn't know God's heart.

Know God's heart, and He'll give you His secrets. Show God that you can be a good steward of those secrets. Show God that you will act in love, compassion, and supernatural power, and He'll start revealing secrets to you. If you just want to act in power like Joram, without love, then God receives no glory.

The disciples James and John had this problem. Some towns rejected Jesus's message, and they said, "Shall we call down fire on them?" (Luke 9:54). They wanted to use supernatural power in a way that was antithetical to love. God is not going to receive glory from that.

But then there's the person who *does* nothing. God isn't excited to reveal secrets to that person either, because there needs to be action.

Is the secret just a source of spiritual pride for you? Is it only useful when you want it to be useful? That's really selfish, and God's not cool with that. Know God's heart, and He'll give you His secrets. Then, use God's secrets with God's love and power, and God receives glory. That is good stewardship that clears the way for more. Do something with the secrets God gives you. What have you done with the things God has already told you?

"Do not kill them," he answered. "Would you kill those you have captured with your own sword or bow? Set food and water before them so that they may eat and drink and then go back to their master." So he prepared a great feast for them, and after they had finished eating and drinking, he sent them away, and they returned to their master. So the bands from Aram stopped raiding Israel's territory. (2 Kings 6:22–23)

Do you want to know how to stop raiding? Or do you want to make the war worse? Do you want to know the purpose of this whole thing? Peace is the purpose. In fact, not only was peace achieved through the prophet Elisha, but there were many in Aram who believed in the God of Israel. There were so many believers in Aram that Elisha—not the prophets of their god—*Elisha* was the one to anoint the next King of Aram.

So this wasn't a party trick for Elisha. It's tied to the fruit of the Spirit and the primary purposes of God in the world. Words of knowledge are always purposeful.

DISCUSS/REFLECT

Have you ever asked God for supernatural knowledge? What happened? What has kept you from asking more often?

_____

_____

_____

_____

_____

What secrets of your heart need to be handled by God? How can you become a better steward of the secrets of other people's heart?

_____

_____

_____

_____

STUDY

Reread the passage in 2 Kings 6:8–23.

What stirred in your spirit as you read? How did God speak to you?

_____

_____

_____

_____

Why do you think Elijah was the only one hearing the words of knowledge? How did this give him influence?

_____

_____

_____

_____

_____

EXERCISE

Ask God for supernatural knowledge (a word of knowledge) for someone right now. Write their name down. Then ask God what He wants to share about them (for their benefit). Ask God what He wants you to do with that information. Pray for God's love as you share that with them. And share with humility, asking if it's true. Admit you're still learning to hear God and seek to verify if you're hearing correctly.

Chapter 19 –
Healing Foundations

The first two sections of the book spent so much time on healing that only a little more will be said here. Suffice to say that physical healing was central to Jesus's life and ministry, and it's easy for the believer. Healing is a "prove it" kind of a demonstration of God's power in the Bible, and it shows that God is alive and active.

POWER OUTAGE

Lights turned out on over 300 kids in the middle of our worship set. No sound. I was almost the only adult in the room (my worship team was teenagers, and the other camp counselors were in a counselors meeting). Kid's camp was about to get WILD! Blood pressure went up for everyone in the room. Panic-mode was loaded and ready!

But God had been burning in my heart exactly what needed to happen next. I put my guitar down and started yelling out over the crowd of 1ˢᵗ–6ᵗʰ Graders: "God wants to do something awesome right now! Who in the room has pain or sickness?"

About 70 hands went up.

"Everyone else, go to someone with their hand up and start praying for healing. Don't pray wimpy prayers . . ."

About 15 minutes later, the adults started filtering back into the room. They were a little bewildered. Lights had come back on, and there was a line of children coming up to the stage and telling about how God had healed them that morning. That morning Jesus healed 100% of the kids who were sick or in pain! Not one left with sickness or pain that day! Jesus is amazing! Only Jesus!

So much of the Christian church lives in a spiritual power outage, and God is calling us to light up His world with healing.

THE ONE WHO MATTERS

One night, as I was about to teach on healing, Holy Spirit said to me, "Lead them to the Healer." Because, bottom line: All healing flows from the blood of Jesus.

In the Old Testament, healing was very rare and often related to a "man of power." In the New Testament, healing is not rare. It's almost automatic. A major change took place when Jesus came. All comes from Jesus. Healing is always about the Healer.

Watch Jesus work here:

> When evening came, many who were demon-
> possessed were brought to him, and he drove out the spirits

with a word and healed *all* the sick. This was to fulfill what was spoken through the prophet Isaiah:

"He *took up* our infirmities
and *bore* our diseases."
(Matthew 8:16–17, emphasis added)

Matthew expertly quoted Isaiah 53 (about the "Suffering Servant") here, showing that healing was solidified in Jesus's atoning work. The destruction of Jesus's body is the prophetic opposite of the healing of yours. The Holy Spirit, through this Scripture, invites you to imagine the pain Jesus went through, and the more pain He went through, the more your pain, sickness, disease, infirmity *has* to leave. That's why communion is a great tool in praying for healing.

HEALING AND GOD'S WILL

I believe that God's perfect will is to heal. His perfect will is being done in heaven, where there is no sickness or disease; and we're told to pray heaven to earth. Jesus never *asked* God if He was willing to heal.

There was a leper in Luke 5 and Matthew 8 who came to Jesus and said, "If you're willing, you can make me clean." Jesus touched him and said, "I am willing. Be clean!"

Jesus never "sicked" anyone; He healed them. He never blessed any storms. He never said, "That's to teach them patience."

Nope! *NEVER!* Read the Bible; you'll know. He just healed everyone!

Why do people not get healed sometimes? Specifically, I don't know. Generally, though, it's the fall of man. Sin entered the world, and everything got messed up. Sin now touches everything, and not fairly. The world is a mess. The "why" goes all the way back to the Garden of Eden. Since then, everything here moves toward more and more chaos.

But there's a better question we should be asking—one we *must* be asking: Why would God step into time and space and change the natural order of things from decay and death to healing? Why would God heal someone? The answer is because He's real, He's love, and He desperately wants relationship to be restored with you and with everyone. Healing is one way the Holy Spirit wants to manifest Himself to our world.

So command earth to look like heaven. Don't pray wimpy prayers for healing; that is not Biblical. Wimpy prayer won't work anyway. When you're clothed in powered by the Holy Spirit, declare healing. I believe the Father's like, "That's My boy! He's acting like His older brother Jesus!"

Pray like Jesus, and your results will be more and more like Jesus.

PRAY WITH JESUS

Jesus does not want your begging. Sure, He'll listen—and you can be sure that He'll still steward your little heart well and with compassion; but He has no need for groveling. Let me say it this way: If you have the choice—if you know better—you might as well pray smarter. Pray like Jesus—like a son or daughter of the King. Pray like someone who *knows* Jesus's compassion and who *knows* their Father's will to do good and not evil. Pray with Jesus, through the power of the Holy Spirit, looking in your Heavenly Father's eyes, and command (with authority) that earth would look like heaven.

What if there's more to prayer than pleading and begging? Demons and people rejecting Jesus know how to plead and beg. Sons and daughters know how to pray.

Do you know how to pray? I'm not saying that in a derogatory way. Do you know how to pray with Jesus—truly converse with Him—through the power of the Holy Spirit, looking in your Heavenly Father's eyes? Do you know how to command with authority that earth would like heaven? It's not ok to stay a baby in this area. You've got to take the next step.

Let me say this one more time. Pray with Jesus. Converse with Him, through the power of the Holy Spirit, looking in your Heavenly Father's eyes; and command with authority that earth would like heaven. That's how the apostles prayed. That's what Jesus modeled. And that's the endgame, the goal, the ideal for every one of us.

THE CERTAINTY OF HEALING

"Would you like prayer for healing?"

"I don't know; I'm skeptical."

"It doesn't matter. Jesus will heal you anyway. What do you have to lose?"

So, we prayed. She was completely healed and testified the next week, "At first I was skeptical, but I can walk now!"

They don't have to have faith. As the believer praying, *you* do. God heals because He wants to prove to people that He's amazing and loves them. So, of course they don't need faith. *They* need the Spirit of God in you!

James 5:15 says, "And the prayer offered in faith will make the sick person well; the Lord will raise them up. If they have sinned, they will be forgiven." God's forgiveness is certain, right? We believe in His forgiveness completely. We come to Him, and He forgives us. *Period.* Here, James echoes Jesus, indicating that our healing is just as certain as God's forgiveness. Jesus made this link many times as well. A statement like this isn't meant to make us feel bad when healing doesn't happen; it's meant to raise our faith up so it *can* happen.

After that, James adds, "Therefore confess your sins to each other and pray for each other so that you may be healed. The prayer of a righteous person is powerful and effective" (James 5:16 NIV). There is a link between right living and answered prayer. Not a one-to-one ratio, but a link. You should always pray for healing. That said, live rightly before God, and you can claim this Scripture too.

PRAY AGAIN

In Mark 8:22, we read, "They came to Bethsaida, and some people brought a blind man and begged Jesus to touch him." The fad of touching Jesus's hem (Mark 6:56) has passed. Now they're on to the next thing: "Jesus, You have to touch us!" But what if the power of Jesus is more than a fad or party trick?

Laying on of hands to pray for healing is good, and there is Biblical precedent for it, so I happily lay hands on sick people to see them healed if I can. However, that is not the only way that people were healed in the Bible. You can send out the word, spit in the mud, command it to go, lift the person up, etc. We are informed by God's Word, but God is not limited by His Word. It's all about Jesus, not the method (especially not this *next* method…).

"He took the blind man by the hand and led him outside the village. When he had spit on the man's eyes and put his hands on him, Jesus asked, "Do you see anything?" (Mark 8:23).

Jesus actively destroys comfort zones. Jesus aggressively crushed people's comfort zones throughout His life, like it was His job. He is not neutral on this. Why? Because your comfort zone keeps you from the "more" Jesus has for you.

Some of you have built up walls around your experience with God—it has to look and feel and smell like this or that, or else God hasn't moved. Those are comfort zones, and they're keeping you from the "more" of God. So, Jesus is trying to destroy that, but we have a tendency to call that discomfort the work of "the enemy." The very discomfort that offers a breakthrough has become a stumbling block for the one who refuses God's work. Allow Jesus to be Lord in your life and to invade your comfort zone however He wants.

Back to the blind man. Jesus spit in his eyes and asked him what he saw. "He looked up and said, 'I see people; they look like trees walking around.' *Once more* Jesus put his hands on the man's eyes. Then his eyes were opened, his sight was restored, and he saw everything clearly" (Mark 8:24–25, emphasis added).

Pray again. This is your permission to pray against sickness and pain multiple times. If you pray once and there's change, pray again and see it completed. If you pray and there's no change, pray again. …and again.

Look, if Jesus had to pray twice for something, I might have to pray a hundred times. When is the time to stop? When the love-meter in the situation has expired, or the Holy Spirit tells you something specific that would require stopping, like "They're going to be healed as they walk away." Or "don't touch this, I'm going to handle it." Four times, the Bible records that people were healed "as they went." In other words, the healing wasn't instant, but it soon became complete. But as long as there's willingness from the person, the Holy Spirit, and you, then it's time to press in.

STAY ON MISSION

"And one of them struck the servant of the high priest, cutting off his right ear. But Jesus answered, 'No more of this!' And he touched the man's ear and healed him" (Luke 22:50–51).

If you want to keep living from earth's perspective, you'll get earthly results. If you're willing to listen to heaven's perspective, then you'll get heaven's results. For Jesus, in this moment in the garden, it wasn't about a revolution; it was about obedience to His Father. It was about caring for the person directly in front of Him, who in this case wanted to kill Him.

Jesus never gave up His mission to heal and save. Even when people were trying to kill Him, He kept on healing and saving. We know this is the High Priest's servant, and we know this his name is Malchus. Why do we know all that about him? The most likely explanation is that he became a Christian later. Jesus kept inviting people in, even to His last breath—even in spite of the worst treatment—because He knew His mission. Jesus was clear on His marching orders. He was constantly with His Father.

Prayer enables you to stay on mission. What's the mission that *you* need to pray into? Being a better co-worker, a better husband, better wife, better father, mother, friend, son, daughter, a better Christian?

Pray … and stay on mission. With God's help, heal and save those around you.

DISCUSS/REFLECT

What have been your experiences in praying for healing? How is God reworking and resetting you to pray in the future?

_____

_____

_____

_____

_____

Have you ever seen someone healed physically? How does healing prove Jesus' good work on the earth?

_____

_____

_____

_____

_____

STUDY

Read Matthew 8:1–17 (Jesus heals, a lot).

What stirred in your spirit as you read? How did God speak to you?

_____

_____

_____

_____

_____

How many different ways did Jesus heal? What do you think a healing revival like this would do to people today?

EXERCISE

Pray for healing right now. Start with yourself. Then move on to friends and family. Be bold. Call or text them. Also remember, *nothing's* too small for God. He wants to receive glory from every sniffle-healing and every wart falling off.

The New "Normal"

It was another complaining person. In my head, I started complaining about all the complaining I was hearing (ironic, right?). There were no warm fuzzies—no particular spiritual vibe— just internal eyerolls (am I allowed to be real for a moment?).

Then it dawned on me. All this complaining was about physical pain. I know someone who can help with that!

Alright, here we go (not knowing if they believe in this): "Can I pray for your pain? . . . Right now?"

Their tone softened, "Well . . . sure."

My hand met their shoulder . . . Simple prayer . . . Jesus heals. Everything changes.

Imagine if this were normal for every believer. We wouldn't have enough room in the churches for all the people coming to faith. We wouldn't feel the need to argue family members into godliness. We would be able to look people in the eye, love them fully, and then back it up with the raw, authentic power of God. No need to feel nervous.

What if the supernatural was normal? It was for Jesus, and it was for the early church. And it is becoming that way for so many today.

Here are 3 ways to make the supernatural normal . . .

1. Normal, as in, not weird. Believers were normal in their approach, normal in the flow of conversation and daily activities on their way to supernatural events. The only thing weird about the encounter was generally the miracle itself. When our approach is friendly and genuine, boldness is easy. It's hard for people to get angry at you when you care enough to notice their pain. Asking them if you can pray for it is only somewhat shocking, because it's actually kind.

2. Normal, as in, consistent in occurrence. As we learn to act like New Testament believers, the supernatural will happen with consistency through us (Acts 4:29–33). There was a rhythm and atmosphere of supernatural events that occurred in the early church. When we steward miracles well through testimonies, we will be ready for more.

3. Normal, as in, outside the church. By far, most of the miracles in the New Testament happened outside the church, in the marketplace. Whatever we do inside the church, then, must look, feel, and smell like it would at the supermarket, coffee shop, or our neighbor's driveway.

Chapter 20 –
Normal, as in, Not Weird

There's *good*-weird and *bad*-weird. Jesus was weird to the whole world but in a way that produced life transformations. He was spiritually attractive. His approach was normal, not off-putting. He used normal illustrations for huge spiritual concepts. He had normal conversations that turned into supernatural encounters.

You're designed to be a thermostat, not a thermometer. You're called to set the climate and the temperature around you, not to become your environment. Thermometers are *status-quo*. Thermostats are weird, for better or worse, because they challenge their environment. Is the atmosphere you're producing more like heaven or hell? Are you *good*-weird or *bad*-weird?

Look at this snapshot from Luke's Gospel:

> One Sabbath, when Jesus went to eat in the house of a prominent Pharisee, he was being carefully watched. There

in front of him was a man suffering from abnormal swelling of his body. Jesus asked the Pharisees and experts in the law, "Is it lawful to heal on the Sabbath or not?" But they remained silent. So taking hold of the man, he healed him and sent him on his way. (Luke 14:1–4)

Jesus didn't cater to the spiritual climate of the day; He challenged it. Jesus was attractive to everyone who wanted heaven. Look up how He interacted with people like Nathaniel, the woman at the well, the wedding in Cana, and so on. Everywhere Jesus went, heaven-seekers were normally attracted to Him, and just as normally, the supernatural broke out.

WEIRD DONE WRONG

As a twelve-year-old, I was in a meeting where a woman was acting like she was birthing a baby. That's just inappropriate— know who's in the room. I heard multiple times people shouting negative prophecies in King James English that didn't sit well in anyone's spirit. Then, on a Sunday morning, someone shouted out in tongues (with unbelievers in the room), and no one interpreted (because it wasn't from God that time). The pastor (my dad) taught the church through that mess beautifully, but the outburst was wrong.

I've had evangelists try to physically push me over many times so I would "fall under the power" (*their* power). Holy Spirit doesn't need your help, bro! What if God wants to work differently in the room? There'd be no need to fake it if the authentic power of God were at work.

There were *good*-weird, wild meetings too. I loved wild meetings, like when a prophet would wander around a room, looking for someone to pounce on with a prophetic word. There were times when people were falling all over each other under the power of God—shaking, shouting, running, dancing, jerking, and laughing. But everyone in the room was on board with the Holy Spirit mayhem, and good fruit was coming from it!

However, some people are *too* weird. As a pastor, I have to lovingly help people evaluate that. Turn the mirror on your life and your church life. Maybe *your* weird does not match *Jesus's* weird. Here's a good litmus test: If you don't know any Christians who are *too* weird, it's probably you.

If heaven-seekers are not attracted to your weird, you're probably not Jesus's kind of weird. If you constantly find yourself at odds with your spiritual authorities (the leaders God has placed in your life, with whom you have basic theological agreement), you're probably not Jesus's kind of weird. If you feel that the voice of God in your heart is consistently asking you to do things that violate the laws of love and peace, you need to recalibrate your ears to God's voice. If you feel that the voice of God in your heart is consistently asking you to do things that are not bearing fruit (or bearing negative fruit), you probably need to reevaluate how you are hearing from God.

I'm not saying this to discourage you. Instead, I'm inviting you into the authentic. I promise you there's more! There's plenty of *good*-weird to go around. That's exciting! God has an authentic, supernatural Christianity for you that looks your world in the face and reveals Jesus's heart well.

BECOMING JESUS'S NORMAL

Jesus's "normal" was such that the only weird thing about an interaction with Him was the supernatural power of God. We're invited into that sort of "weird." No need to sound super spiritual, put on a show, or push for a certain way of God manifesting. Instead, trust, listen, obey, and let Holy Spirit do the heavy lifting. Look people in the eye, see them how God sees them, love them with Jesus's love, and meet their needs with the authentic power of God.

THE CASE FOR WEIRD

What about the excess? What about the sin? What about the people who are manifesting in ways that are not from God?

Yeah? What about it? Everyone is manifesting *something*. Every church has excess. Churches who do not have expressive excess simply don't have their excesses out in the open so they can deal with it.

Walk into in any "frozen chosen" (their words, not mine!) style church, and you will find excess—from the guy lusting after the girl two rows ahead as she worships, to the girl sitting in the pew harboring their faulty views of grace, to the person praying faithless prayers to manipulate God rather than honor Him. Excess is possible—nay, *probable*—in every church gathering. If you find a perfect church, don't join—you'll ruin it.[13]

So, there's a case for weird—a case to be made that excessive expressions of the presence of God are actually helpful to the body of Christ, in the big picture. If the nonsense in the Corinthian church wasn't visible, Paul never could have corrected it. You cannot steer a ship that's not moving. When God's moving in a room—and, more specifically, on the hearts and lives of individuals—human flesh sometimes doesn't know what to do with that. So people manifest. And sometimes it's ugly, jarring, and off-putting. Can God still work in that environment? Absolutely. The Day of Pentecost testifies to that (Acts 2).

Some of you aren't weird enough. You're addicted to normal—not the "normal" of the world, necessarily, but perhaps the "normal" of the sanitized church world.

Jesus's kind of weird was very particular—attractive to heaven-seekers in the world, yet supernatural in every way. If all the Christians around you are weird and you're the only "normal" one, you're probably not weird enough. If you've never had anyone accuse you of being drunk when you're experiencing God (Acts 2:13), you're not weird enough. If you've never had anyone who needs to be healed or delivered from demons think to ask *you* for

---

[13] Somebody said this concept before me, but its originator is unknown.

help, you're not weird enough. If you're not constantly asking the Father, "How do You want me to act or talk to this person?" you're not weird like Jesus. Jesus said, I only do what I see my Father doing (John 5:19). Your brand of "normal" is not supernatural enough and needs to line up with Jesus's normal.

THE NEW NORMAL

"The place where they were meeting was shaken, and they were all filled with the Holy Spirit" (Acts 4:31). To those who embrace the "frozen chosen" identity: Would you even be available if this happened to your church? It's easy to say an intellectual "yes" to a question like this; but truly, does your practice have room for such an experience?

To those who lean toward Corinthian wildness: Are your gatherings even accessible to outsiders? Are skeptics able to understand what you're saying and doing (1 Cor 14:16)?

To those who think you're sitting right in the middle: When was the last time someone walked into your gathering (church service, life group, personal prayer time, etc.) and, "convicted by all, convinced of all, the secrets of their heart revealed, and falling on their face, they worship God, shouting, 'God is really among you!'" (1 Cor. 14:24–25 JST)?

There's room for growth for all of us, right? The new normal is that our lives and churches would look more and more like the life and ministry of Jesus. Learn Jesus today.

DISCUSS/REFLECT

Have you seen the supernatural done wrong? How are you able to see God's work still in that situation and redeem it in your own heart?

_____

_____

_____

_____

_____

_____

_____

_____

_____

How often do you pray with your neighbors, coworkers, strangers, etc.? Make a list of people you will ask to pray with this week.

_____

_____

_____

_____

_____

_____

_____

STUDY

Read Acts 2 (Day of Pentecost).

What stirred in your spirit as you read? How did God speak to you?

_____

_____

_____

_____

_____

How did Peter's preaching redeem the weirdness? How did the lives of the first Christians reflect Jesus in normal and supernatural ways (Acts 2:41-47)?

_____

_____

_____

_____

_____

_____

EXERCISE

Pray for God to give you a "normal" conversation in the next 24 hours where you can ask someone to pray with you. Pray about the conversation ahead of time. Allow Holy Spirit to show Himself powerfully.

Chapter 21 –

Normal, as in, Consistent in Occurrence

Church gatherings ought to be training grounds for ministry that would work outside the four walls. The way I pray for people at the altar in church is the same way I pray for people at a restaurant or my doctor's office.

Philip, whose story we read in Acts 8, was not an apostle. There is this weird and non-Biblical teaching that only apostles did miracles in the New Testament; and, well, this is one of the many stories that definitively crushes that nonsense. God's call to advance His work is for all believers; it's not a professional clergy thing. If you've committed your life to Christ and you really know Him—and you want the world to know Him—the Holy Spirit wants to work through you. Do you need to be a pastor to for pray someone at a restaurant or your doctor's office? The supernatural should be consistent among all believers.

> When the crowds heard Philip and saw the signs he performed, they all paid close attention to what he said. For with shrieks, impure spirits came out of many, and many who were paralyzed or lame were healed. So there was great joy in that city. (Acts 8:6–8)

The supernatural brings joy. Let's not be concerned about people's reactions prior to them reacting. We don't need to be shy about the supernatural just to manage reactions. It's time for American Christians to realize what is winning, both here and around the world.

We are part of a global movement that is winning. Take this thought to work with you. Take this thought to the supermarket with you, into the restaurants with you, into your personal anxious thoughts.

The number of Christians around the world is growing. The percentage of the world population who are Christians is growing. There are 2.3 billion Christians worldwide, and the number is growing fast with new converts (not merely population growth, like Islam). We get so tunnel-visioned on the problems in American government and the pervasive cultural and media opposition. We get discouraged by the reported overall decline of American Christianity. But see this: Charismatic and Pentecostal Christianity (the kind I'm discussing in this book) is on the rise, both in America and worldwide. In other words, the number of people who believe in and practice the supernatural are increasing daily. The number of miracle-working Christians in the world in 1900 was less than 1 million and is presently 650 million; and we're on pace to break 1 billion in the next 30 years.[14] Miracles are not rare. They are becoming more and more consistent as the gospel advances Spirit-filled Christianity around the world.

Global Christianity is evangelizing Western Christianity with Biblical doctrine about miracles. Mainline denominations are sending out missionaries who are coming back Pentecostal. They're starting churches with "Baptist" and "Methodist" in their name, only to realize when they go to visit their overseas brothers and sisters that these churches are seeing countless miracles. It's undeniable. Secular sociologists who are willing to do unbiased research are finding the supernatural at work in the most caring and growing churches around the world.[15] It is normal for the supernatural to be consistent.

Don't overthink this. Miracles should happen regularly. They should not be rare for the Church of believers who are filled with Holy Spirit. Holy Spirit loves doing what only He can do. The supernatural works of God were part of the regular rhythm of

---

[14] Keener, Craig. *Miracles: The Credibility of the New Testament Accounts*, Vol. 1. (Baker Academic, 2011).
[15] For example, Miller and Yamamori's book *Global Pentecostalism*.

Jesus's ministry and just as much part of the early church—as ordinary and consistent as breathing. Just read the Gospels and Acts; you'll get it. No agenda—just the plain meaning of the text, noting the author's intent in communicating to the original audience.

If my experience doesn't line up with the Word of God, it's not the Bible that's wrong—it's my experience. We're supposed to see the supernatural as a distinctive and normal part of the Christian life. You have permission to long for more of the supernatural in your life.

DISCUSS/REFLECT

How can you raise the consistency of the supernatural work of God in your life? Who are people you can pray for today?

_____

_____

_____

_____

What churchy biases do you need to lay down in order to have a Biblical understanding of the supernatural?

_____

_____

_____

_____

STUDY

Read Acts 8:1–13 (Philip in Samaria).

What stirred in your spirit as you read? How did God speak to you?

_____

_____

_____

_____

_____

What attracted Simon the Sorcerer to the Gospel (v 13)? What walls can be broken down in your city when the authentic supernatural is active?

_____

_____

_____

_____

_____

_____

EXERCISE

Pray with someone every day this week. If you don't find someone randomly, prepare a fallback list of people you know who you can call or visit and pray something "impossible" for them.

Chapter 22 –
Normal, as in, Outside the Church

Jesus did His miracles outside the church, or outside of a formal religious gathering. I went and scanned the 4 Gospels, looking for the setting of every miracle that Jesus did. There are 96 miracle narratives of Jesus recorded in the Gospels, and only 8 of them happened in a synagogue—a formal religious gathering. Another 14 of them happened in unofficial gatherings (like the feeding of the 5000, where people found Jesus in the wilderness).

But 74 of the 96 miracle narratives—or 77%—took place while Jesus was out and about. Almost 4 in 5 of them were completely outside of a religious meeting! The places these miracles happened were in the marketplace (like a supermarket or a restaurant), homes, roads, wells, the foot of a mountain, the shore of a lake, a boat, the wilderness, a solitary place where people found Him, and so on. One of my favorites is when He interrupted a funeral procession (Luke 7:11–17).

The most common place that miracles happened in the Gospels was on the road as Jesus was traveling somewhere. Are you too busy to see the miracles that need to happen around you? Are you moving too fast to see people and have compassion for their needs? Do you feel too important or self-focused to stop and engage the people around you?

What if you treated your travel like Jesus did?

Our focus as believers ought to be to model, internalize, train, and give tools for seeing God work in supernatural ways—ways that will also work outside the church. If our ministry methods won't work with a lost person at Walmart, we ought to adjust those methods, even within our church meetings (where Christians learn to minister to their world). The right approach will fix people's attention on Jesus, not on us or our weird methods. The only things that should freak people out is that the prayer worked, and their lives are now changed for the better. That's how Jesus did it.

POSITION YOURSELF

> Now he had to go through Samaria. So he came to a town in Samaria called Sychar, near the plot of ground Jacob had given to his son Joseph. Jacob's well was there, and Jesus, tired as he was from the journey, sat down by the well. It was about noon. (John 4:4–6)

Jesus was on a journey. This was nothing crazy or special for Him. But Jesus placed Himself intentionally in a spot where He could see and be seen.

Position yourself to interact with people outside the church. If, when we are out, we are always in such a hurry that we aren't looking at the people around us, observing their needs, then we will never be able to see their need or ask questions that open the conversation to looking them in the eye and having a real opportunity to share God's love.

Alternatively, sometimes we're so focused on the people next to us (which is a good thing) that we miss the opportunity to connect with those around us. I believe that it's possible to do both.

"When a Samaritan woman came to draw water, Jesus said to her, 'Will you give Me a drink?' (His disciples had gone into the town to buy food)" (John 4:7–8). Notice Jesus's posture—lounging at the well, the meeting place of the town. He conveyed, "I'm open for conversation." The woman was forced to come into His space. And his question was perfect. In this culture, that was a social question, like, "Hey, would you care to join me for a drink?"—not in an awkward, date-y way, but in a friendly "I would like to get to know you" way.

The question also broke down racial barriers. Jews normally didn't associate with Samaritans. The principle for us is that we can ask questions that are disarming.

INTENTIONAL CONVERSATION

Try this: If you are in the check-out line, or ordering food, or buying something, and a nearby person makes eye contact with you, and there's time: Stop, look them in the eye, and ask with the tone that expects a real answer, "How are you doing?" You will be amazed at the responses. Some people might just bare their souls to you. The key is, you have to take the time and be fully engaged with them enough to look them in the eye and truly care how they respond. You have to be ready to tell them something that will infuse hope, because if they do open up, it's likely *because* they need hope.

> The Samaritan woman said to him, "You are a Jew and I am a Samaritan woman. How can you ask me for a drink?" (For Jews do not associate with Samaritans.) Jesus answered her, "If you knew the gift of God and who it is that asks you for a drink, you would have asked him and he would have given you living water." (John 4:9–10)

Here Jesus is baiting her to deepen the conversation. Good form! And she took the bait. Well played, Jesus.

> "Sir," the woman said, "you have nothing to draw with and the well is deep. Where can you get this living water? Are you greater than our father Jacob, who gave us the well and drank from it himself, as did also his sons and his

livestock?" Jesus answered, "Everyone who drinks this water will be thirsty again, but whoever drinks the water I give them will never thirst. Indeed, the water I give them will become in them a spring of water welling up to eternal life." (John 4:11–14)

Jesus masterfully avoids a direct answer. He *sort of* answers, but He figures out a way to focus on what really matters, all the while baiting her further.

> The woman said to him, "Sir, give me this water so that I won't get thirsty and have to keep coming here to draw water."
> He told her, "Go, call your husband and come back."
> "I have no husband," she replied. (John 4:15–17)

Next, Jesus gave her a word of knowledge about her love life. But He did it in a way that was normal and that furthered the conversation. Suddenly the woman wanted Him to teach her. She sought Him out for more insight. Why? Because the supernatural power of God was present! But that never would have happened if Jesus hadn't approached the conversation in a completely normal way.

> The woman said, "I know that Messiah" (called Christ) "is coming. When he comes, he will explain everything to us."

Then Jesus declared, "I, the one speaking to you—I am he." (John 4:25–26)

Jesus's teaching only *followed* the supernatural. Jesus only offered the woman spiritual insight when He knew her heart was open. When did her heart open? When He blew her mind with a word of knowledge. That's why the supernatural work of God is such a necessity in the church. 86% of the conversion stories in the New Testament contain the supernatural.[16]

DO SOMETHING

Next, we see her reaction:

Then, leaving her water jar, the woman went back to the town and said to the people, "Come, see a man who told me everything I ever did. Could this be the Messiah?" They came out of the town and made their way toward him. (John 4:28–30)

The woman became Jesus's biggest evangelist. Why? Because Jesus showed her something she'd never seen before: the raw, authentic power of the living God, coupled with beautiful love.

---

[16] Check out my Doctoral Dissertation for all the data and references: https://jaredstepp.files.wordpress.com/2019/05/making_the_supernatural_normal_jared_stepp_doctoral_project.pdf

As the woman evangelized the town, Jesus taught His disciples a principle of being naturally supernatural. He said, "My food is to do the will of Him who sent me and to finish His work" (John 4:34).

It's all about the doing. Go do it. Solid food is doing the work of God. Milk is hearing the word; solid food is doing. We don't stop needing milk just because we start eating solid food; however, if we're ever going to actually grow, then solid food becomes a bigger and bigger part of our diet. It's the same with spiritual things. We will continue to need to hear the Word our entire lives. It's just that we will be spiritual runts—spiritual infants in adult bodies—until we start on the solid food of *doing* God's work.

Don't worry about whether or not you'll close the deal (meaning pray the salvation prayer with them, or see them over the moon excited when they get healed). Simply start doing the work! The more people you love with the supernatural, the more likely you are to see amazing results.

Let's see how the woman responded:

> Many of the Samaritans from that town believed in him because of the woman's testimony, "He told me everything I ever did." So when the Samaritans came to him, they urged him to stay with them, and he stayed two days. And because of his words many more became believers.

They said to the woman, "We no longer believe just because of what you said; now we have heard for ourselves, and we know that this man really is the Savior of the world." (John 4:39–42)

DISCUSS/REFLECT

How can you practice in your church to pray for people outside the church? How does attitude change the way you interact with people at church?

_____

_____

_____

_____

_____

What are some modern "wells"—places where people gather? How can you position yourself in people's paths at these places?

_____

_____

_____

_____

_____

_____

_____

STUDY

Reread John 4:6–43 (Woman at the Well).

What stirred in your spirit as you read? How did God speak to you?

_____

_____

_____

_____

_____

_____

Verse 6 says Jesus was tired and lounging. How can you turn your rest and lounging into a space for God to receive glory? Does God want to remake or relocate your rest?

_____

_____

_____

_____

_____

EXERCISE

Pray that God will give you a time, place, and conversation in which you can pray with people outside the church this week. Imagine the room you'll be in. Imagine the kinds of conversations that you can turn toward prayer. Ask God to make it easy.

CONCLUSION

Congratulations on working through this book and the discussions and exercises in it! I believe this is a catalyst in your life to more growth than you could imagine. I'm declaring health in your soul, body, and mind. I bless you to experience upgrades in the Spirit from now until you go to be with Jesus permanently.

Take the time to look back and work through any of the reflection/discussions and, especially, exercises that you may have missed along the way. The gold is in the doing.

Take at least one risk with God every day. Ask God for words or pictures. Call or text people with the things He shows you. Approach a stranger and ask if you can pray for them. Approach a friend or family member and ask if you can pray. Ask Holy Spirit for divinely set up appointments with people, then walk in obedience to them. Ask God for visions and dreams, then learn with Him how to discern, act on them, and convey the messages to others.

For many of you, this next season will be the most amazing season of walking with God in your life to this point. You're going to be able to recognize His voice consistently, which means you will also hear Him more.

As you see the supernatural works of God grow in your life, tell people about them. Give God praise! Your testimonies will clear the way for more of God's works in your life, and they'll be the ground that others needed for their own breakthroughs. Steward the gold of those testimonies well.

God is making the supernatural normal in your world!

APPENDIX A:

Frequently Asked Questions

(Not a comprehensive list)

DO I NEED TO BE BAPTIZED IN THE HOLY SPIRIT?

No. But also, yes.

Let me explain.

> On one occasion, while he was eating with them, he gave them this command: "Do not leave Jerusalem, but wait for the gift my Father promised, which you have heard me speak about. (Acts 1:4)

The gift (Holy Spirit baptism) isn't just from Jesus—it's from God the Father too. God is fully in on this—all three Persons of the Trinity have the same mind. This also reminds us that Jesus didn't say anything or do anything that God the Father didn't tell Him to say or do.

God the Holy Spirit is fully unified in purpose and essence with God the Father and God the Son. They are three distinct Persons in personality and function but one God in essence, character, and purpose. It's such an awesome mystery. We don't fully understand God just yet. There's still mystery, there's still wonder, there's still awe-inspiring majesty. There's still more. There is more of God for you.

The Biblical pattern is to be saved (Holy Spirit *IN* you), water baptized, and baptized in Holy Spirit (Holy Spirit *ON* you), which comes with the physical evidence of speaking in a spiritual language we haven't learned.

I have no trouble imagining that it's possible there are other initial evidences of the baptism in Holy Spirit. However, there aren't other evidences presented in the Bible. So, if it's ok with you. I'm simple, and I'd like to stick with the one the Bible presents rather than the one's humans imagine.

Jesus regularly talked about Holy Spirit to His disciples. In the opening Scripture above, Jesus said, "…which you have heard me speak about." In other words, Jesus had already been fully invested in giving the disciples power through Holy Spirit. And guess what? Jesus is *still* fully invested in giving us Holy Spirit today.

In the next verse, Jesus continued, "For John baptized with water, but in a few days you will be baptized with the Holy Spirit" (Acts 1:5). Baptism literally means immersion. Jesus prophesied about us soaking in the Holy Spirit. If your clothes are soaked, everyone can see it, and everyone you touch can feel it. Has someone ever tried to give you a hug with soaking wet clothes?

That's what the Baptism in the Holy Spirit is. Holy Spirit, who lives inside of you, is now seen on the outside too. Some of us have not plugged into God's power that way, and people aren't seeing God's power through us. There's more for you today.

Acts 1:7–8 continues, "He said to them: 'It is not for you to know the times or dates the Father has set by his own authority. But you will receive power …'" Jesus spoke of God's authority and jurisdiction first, and then He flowed seamlessly into articulating the authority that God is delegating to us: You will receive power.

Jesus was saying, "There are still some things that are reserved to be mystery, but let Me refocus and prioritize the most important thing for you right now. You've already experienced salvation. Now, this is what you have to focus on. You've already committed your life to Me, and Holy Spirit is inside. This is what's coming. This is your priority. We're not done. There is more.

> But you will receive power when the Holy Spirit comes
> on you; and you will be my witnesses in Jerusalem, and in
> all Judea and Samaria, and to the ends of the earth." After

he said this, he was taken up before their very eyes, and a
cloud hid him from their sight. (Acts 1:8–9)

Holy Spirit comes *on* you. He's already *in* you, and now He's
coming *on* you. There you go: baptism in the Holy Spirit. Jesus is
so consistent with describing this spiritual reality, it's awesome.

Then, in Acts 1:8, the purpose of the baptism in the Holy
Spirit is revealed as power to talk about Jesus. It can't be clearer
from Scripture. This isn't a "bless me" club. Although there is
collateral blessing to us that comes from being baptized in Holy
Spirit, that's not the purpose. The purpose is to bless others, letting
them know that Jesus is alive.

We can talk about Jesus all we want, but until we plug in to
the power of God, it's only going to be talk. I have been running
electrical wire in my basement. I have never run electrical wire
before, but I have zero fear of nailing it up to the wall and feeding
it through holes in the floor joists. I'm comfortable being rough
with it and twisting it around. Why? Because *it's not plugged in to the
power source yet.* It's not tied into the breaker box. As soon as it gets
tied in, there is all of a sudden a HUGE respect for every bit of
that thing. Without any knowledge of it, there is no way I'm
touching that thing. But as long as it's not plugged in, I'll mess with
that cord all I want.

That's how Satan feels about us, as long as we're believers
but not yet fully tied into to the Power Source—Holy Spirit. We
can look, talk, and smell like Christians all we want, but he doesn't

care. The devil will mess with us and beat us up, manipulate us, and shove us out of the way, out of the action, until we tie into to the Power Source. He sees past the façade—he sees past the charade. Satan might be powerless compared to God, but he's not stupid, and he does know where to look. He looks at our connection to Holy Spirit. It's obvious when we're not tied in to power. It shows on the outside. So, he tacks us to the wall where we're out of the way of the actions and are useless to expand God's kingdom.

It's time to tie into the power source.

I've had an atheist and an agnostic try to convert me. They're *really* vocal. They're evangelists for their cause, even though they say they aren't (and even though they lack any good news). But they had a huge problem: they had no power. The one guy tried to speak into my future, like a prophet would, steering me toward being a Broadway vocalist. Really, that was something I was talented at and receiving awards for in high school. The problem was this was never in my heart. There was no confirmation. There was no power. He was simply trying in his own strength to steer me toward anything but God.

When a real prophet speaks into your life, there will be confirmations. There will be power. It will produce good things in your life.

The agnostic's word was impotent. In fact, directly after that, that next year, I quit my Broadway musical involvements—to the great angst of all my directors, who had wanted to pick a musical with a lead part just for me. But God was preparing me for this. I know what it looks like when a prophetic word really rings true.

Next, the baptism in the Holy Spirit is not automatic at salvation. It was always and consistently a second distinct work in Scripture. Have you ever thought, "There's more?" Have you ever been hungry for more in your spiritual life? That hunger is placed there by God. It was there from when He first formed Adam out of dust. He stamped His image on us, and now we want more of Him, constantly. That desire will only grow until we reach heaven.

God will still do miracles from time to time in the life of a believer who has not been baptized in the Holy Spirit. It is much like miracles happened in the Old Testament from time to time. Holy Spirit would descend for a particular moment and then leave. However, the New Testament pattern is different. Plugging into God's power is better.

Now, here's the payoff. What happened when Holy Spirit came?

> When the day of Pentecost came, they were all together in one place. Suddenly a sound like the blowing of a violent wind came from heaven and filled the whole house where they were sitting. They saw what seemed to be tongues of fire that separated and came to rest on each of them. All of them were filled with the Holy Spirit and began to speak in other tongues as the Spirit enabled them. (Acts 2:1–4)

A crowd gathered thinking they were drunk. Then Peter preached in power, and 3,000 people got saved—along with miracles and the supernatural that continued as a part of the believers' culture.

Speaking in tongues is a language you've never learned or studied. Tongues weren't meant to be weird. And it's not Holy Spirit possessing you and taking over your tongue. Instead, it is a directing of spiritual language from your own spirit as you partner with the Holy Spirit.

These details are irrelevant to your seeking because they were irrelevant to the first believers. But I share them to remove excuses and misconceptions so you can freely seek God for more.

Bottom line: You can still be full-in on Jesus—saved, growing in the fruit of the Spirit (His internal work), and even see a miracle from time to time—without being baptized in the Holy Spirit. However, you'll never make the supernatural normal in your life, your church, or your world unless you're plugged into the power of God through Holy Spirit Baptism.

WHAT ABOUT WHEN AN OBVIOUS MIRACLE HAPPENS BUT THEN PAIN COMES BACK?

Many times, this is an invitation to contend for the miracle. God doesn't need you to cover for Him. You can be authentic about what happened. Instead, get back in that place with the Lord and pray again.

Also, consider that the pain coming back in some way does not discount the fact that it left when you prayed the first time. Sometimes, there are lifestyle issues that need to be considered in bringing pain back. God can give you insight into those so that the healing will stay. Contend. At the same time, until eternity, all healing is technically temporary. We celebrate every healing as it comes; and when it doesn't, we contend.

DO MY PRAYERS EXPIRE?

"Our baby has Trisomy 13. We came to you for help." *WOAH!* That's a lot of pressure! But I knew exactly what they were talking about. Trisomy 13 is a rare genetic disease that is a death sentence to babies within the first year of life. The doctors had suspected that our son Jaren had it, and so we had prayed against it, in loud and passionate prayer meetings with extended family for weeks. Then he was tested, and we found out that he never had it in the first place. We guessed our prayers were wasted or had expired. The termination point for those prayers had come and gone. We had wasted our time.

Or had we?

What if our prayers didn't expire?

Now, this couple's son *did* have this horrific death sentence. They had heard about Jaren coming back from death multiple times and had come to us rather than having an abortion like the doctors suggested. We asked if the doctors were sure, and they said they were 100% positive.

Something strange happened in that moment. We didn't have to reach for extra faith. We didn't have to drum up emotion. Jessica's and my prayers were locked and loaded. We contended in the Spirit with them for a few minutes and declared life, just as we had so many times with our own son. There was a sense of breakthrough—everyone knew it.

The Bible records a church prayer meeting in Acts 12 that was demoralized and faithless. The church had prayed powerfully and passionately for James the apostle when Herod took him, but he died. So, the night before Peter's trial, the church was praying, but no one was believing the way they had for James. The Bible records that even when Peter showed up at their door, they weren't believing it!

But what if their prayers for James hadn't expired?

Was Peter more important than James, and that's why this happened? No. Did God "need another angel," and so He picked James to take him to heaven? *Definitely* not. What happened to James was simply natural life in a fallen world. However, Peter's deliverance provided hope. It raised the tide of faith again, and a surge of people came into the church (Acts 12:24).

Back to the baby in our story. Three months later, their son was born completely healthy! The incurable had been cured by the Great Physician! The doctors were scrambling to figure out what had happened. His chromosomes had gone back to normal.

So, your prayers for a job, a relationship, or a healing may seem like they have expired. But did they? I would encourage you to go back to those places of passionate prayer in your spirit and allow God to infuse your prayer life now with renewed faith. I believe that God has a purpose in that process and that those prayers are still ready to produce in your life for the next situation. Allow God to rebuild your faith right now.

WHY, GOD?

"Hi, Laura! How are you?" I asked, answering my cell phone.

"Well, Tim passed away last night."

She was devastated. I was stunned. He was my friend and was 44, the father of 8 kids—a man of intense, beautiful faith and passion for God, his family, and the supernatural. He had been miraculously and completely healed of cancer about 11 months earlier. Then he was diagnosed with an aggressive liver disease that took him out in 3 months.

At that moment in my faith, the "why?" question was unnecessary and even hurtful. I knew why: death, sickness, sin, Satan's works—that's the natural way of things. God gave us dominion over our world, and we gave it away through sin. Jesus restored it, and we are still learning to walk in that authority. God our Father understands loss and even sickness, but He didn't cause it. Here's the principle . . .

Scripture always addresses the "why" question on the positive but not the negative. The negative is obvious—it's natural. The positive, though—well, that's supernatural. That's God's domain.

- **John 9 –** Why was the man born blind? So that God's works might be displayed (healing).
- **Rom 8:28 –** Why do bad things happen? Doesn't matter. God will turn them for good, for those who love Him.

Why did my friend die in the prime of life? Not the right question. God was (and is) miraculously with that family throughout. What about asking why he got healed of cancer and had 11 more months with them? That's a better question.

At the funeral, we cried and sang powerfully the words to Tim's favorite song—"One Thing Remains"—about death, life, and our confidence in God's love. God's presence was so thick and wonderful. Why? Because He loves us, and He thinks we're amazing. He is fully dedicated to orchestrating any natural circumstance into supernatural good.

WHAT ABOUT RECEIVING A NEGATIVE RESPONSE?

"Stretch your hand out!" Those watching scurry to pull their jaws off the floor as the man's shriveled hand becomes wholly functional again.

Dancing in this man's head are the sports events he won't have to miss out on, the earning potential at his job that will increase, and the caresses from his wife that he won't miss. He's overjoyed but realizes something is wrong in the room. He tries desperately to wash the smile off his face, but it doesn't work. Goodness is winning inside him.

Yet he sees the shaking heads, hears the murmurs, and feels cold stares. They were outraged—the "important" people, the ones who ran things. When they got like this, people died. This was not good—and yet, it was *soooo* good. He still couldn't wipe the grin from his face as he hurried out of the room, past "them" and home. Jesus had just been outrageously good to him. Now he had to reconcile that with his life. It was going to be so fun!

Why would we settle for just *normal* good, when we can be *outrageously* good? What if each of us were not just capable of, but committed to, blessing others in outrageously good ways? This was Jesus' M.O.—His signature move. His routine recipe. The woman caught in adultery (John 8), healing the paralytic (Matt 9), Lazarus (John 11), the woman who washed his feet (Luke 7), etc. It wasn't a full day's work if Jesus hadn't ticked someone off with His ridiculous levels of goodness.

What if we became like Jesus in this way? What if *our* crazy matched *His* crazy goodness? This is not just possible; it is the destiny of the body of Christ.

The "sinner" who needs scandalous grace, the stranger who needs an excessive gift, the friend who needs embarrassing praise, the hope for God's best that needs rekindled in us today. Every day is an opportunity to be outrageously good, just like Jesus.

CAN YOU BE TOO HEAVENLY MINDED?

No, but you can be so earthly minded that you're useless in heaven. You can also be so religious sounding that you annoy people in your life (that's *really* what people are getting at when they say this).

I really dislike that phrase now. "So heavenly minded we're of no earthly good." It's just not Biblical. In fact, it's anti-Biblical. Because now, churches have gone so far in the opposite direction that we've stopped remembering that heaven is our home, right now.

The moment we commit our lives to Jesus, the greatest miracle happens: God comes into our lives and takes up residence in our souls. From that moment on, according to the Bible, eternity starts. We have now entered into eternal life.

The theme of Jesus's teaching—the undisputed theme—is the kingdom of heaven. His message declared that the kingdom of heaven is here, and His teaching was constantly telling us what the kingdom of heaven is like. Almost all His parables started that way.

The truth is this: Jesus lived out of a heavenly reality. All believers are called to live out of that same heavenly reality, constantly—in our hearts and spirits—looking in our Father's eyes, knowing His will, knowing He's good, knowing He's smiling on us, and then enforcing His will into earthly problems.

Dallas Willard, an amazing philosopher and theologian who has mentored so many amazing men and women of God, once said that he wondered when he died if it would be awhile before he realized it. That's a picture of living out of the heavenly reality.

Colossians 3:2 teaches us, "Set your minds on things above, not on earthly things."

The Lord's Prayer says, "Our Father, in heaven [that's His home and ours], holy is Your name. Your kingdom come [that's the heavenly kingdom], Your will be done on earth as it is in heaven." God's will is done in heaven, and it's His will for us to pray heaven to earth.

Philippians 3:20 says, "But our citizenship is in heaven. And we eagerly await a Savior from there, the Lord Jesus Christ."

So, how do we achieve this mindset? What is the disconnect? Why are we obsessed with temporal realities, temporal problems and temporal solutions when God is fixated on majesty?

I believe the answer is firmly rooted in Scripture. The answer the Bible gives to living out of a heavenly reality—the answer Jesus gave resoundingly—is, "Be filled with Holy Spirit." This is Jesus's gift to all believers. Jesus gives us Holy Spirit at salvation. The Scripture says that the Spirit of Christ takes up residence in us. At that point, we have all of Holy Spirit inside of us that is possible. However, Jesus didn't stop there. He said, "Be clothed in power." That's a second act.

In John 21, before Jesus left the earth, He breathed on the disciples and said, "Receive the Holy Spirit." That's salvation. That was the moment when the disciples went from being OT believers to being NT believers. That was the moment of conversion where the eternal power of the cross of Jesus was initiated in their lives to save them from hell and for heaven—to save them from sin and for right living, from Satan's power to the presence of God. The Spirit of Jesus Christ on the inside of humans beings … What a miracle! The greatest miracle.

But Jesus wasn't done. Weeks later, He told them, "I'm sending you the Holy Spirit."

"But wait, you already gave us Holy Spirit!"

"Yeah—on the inside. But in order for you to live out the heavenly reality, in order for people to see God's power in you, you're going to have to be 'Clothed in power' (Luke 24:49)."

"Clothed in power" was the language Jesus used. That means the One who lives inside of you can come out so that others can see it and experience God's power upon you, spreading God's kingdom in the earth. And the book of Acts shows us, that's precisely how the kingdom of God did spread on the earth.

Ways God Speaks in Scripture

(Adapted from Ray & Renaid Almgren, Fire for the Nations)

GENERAL SCRIPTURES

Hebrews 1:1–2 – In the past God spoke to our ancestors through the prophets at many times and in various ways, but in these last days he has spoken to us by his Son, whom he appointed heir of all things, and through whom also he made the universe.

Exodus 3:1–4 – Now Moses was tending the flock of Jethro his father-in-law, the priest of Midian, and he led the flock to the far side of the wilderness and came to Horeb, the mountain of God. There the angel of the LORD appeared to him in flames of fire from within a bush. Moses saw that though the bush was on fire it did not burn up. So Moses thought, "I will go over and see this strange sight—why the bush does not burn up." When the LORD saw that he had gone over to look, God called to him from within the bush, "Moses! Moses!" And Moses said, "Here I am."

Acts 26:14 – We all fell to the ground, and I heard a voice saying to me in Aramaic, 'Saul, Saul, why do you persecute me? It is hard for you to kick against the goads.'

Hosea 2:14–15 – "Therefore I am now going to allure her; I will lead her into the wilderness and speak tenderly to her. There I will give her back her vineyards, and will make the Valley of Achor a door of hope. There she will respond as in the days of her youth, as in the day she came up out of Egypt.

SPECIFIC WAYS GOD SPEAKS

1. Creation

Psalm 19:1 – For the director of music. A psalm of David. The heavens declare the glory of God; the skies proclaim the work of his hands.

Romans 1:20 – For since the creation of the world God's invisible qualities—his eternal power and divine nature—have been clearly seen, being understood from what has been made, so that people are without excuse.

2. Small Voice

1 Kings 19:11–12 – The LORD said, "Go out and stand on the mountain in the presence of the LORD, for the LORD is about to pass by." Then a great and powerful wind tore the mountains apart and shattered the rocks before the LORD, but the LORD was not in the wind. After the wind there was an earthquake, but the LORD was not in the earthquake. After the earthquake came a fire, but the LORD was not in the fire. And after the fire came a gentle whisper.

3. Audible Voice

John 12:28–29 – Father, glorify your name!" Then a voice came from heaven, "I have glorified it, and will glorify it again." The crowd that was there and heard it said it had thundered; others said an angel had spoken to him.

4. Revelation (Knowing)

Matthew 16:17 – Jesus replied, "Blessed are you, Simon son of Jonah, for this was not revealed to you by flesh and blood, but by my Father in heaven.

5. A Burning Heart

Luke 24:32 – They asked each other, "Were not our hearts burning within us while he talked with us on the road and opened the Scriptures to us?"

6. Inner Witness

Romans 8:16 – The Spirit himself testifies with our spirit that we are God's children.

7. Dreams

Job 33:15–18 – In a dream, in a vision of the night, when deep sleep falls on people as they slumber in their beds, he may speak in their ears and terrify them with warnings, to turn them from wrongdoing and keep them from pride, to preserve them from the pit, their lives from perishing by the sword.

8. Visions (Pictures or Moving Pictures)

Acts 16:9–10 – During the night Paul had a vision of a man of Macedonia standing and begging him, "Come over to Macedonia and help us." After Paul had seen the vision, we got ready at once to leave for Macedonia, concluding that God had called us to preach the gospel to them.

9. Circumstances (Doors)

Revelation 3:7–8 – "To the angel of the church in Philadelphia write: These are the words of him who is holy and true, who holds the key of David. What he opens no one can shut, and what he shuts no one can open. I know your deeds. See, I have placed before you an open door that no one can shut. I know that you have little strength, yet you have kept my word and have not denied my name.

10. Finances (Provision)

1 Kings 17:7 – Some time later the brook dried up because there had been no rain in the land.

11. "Handwriting on the Wall" (Signs)

Daniel 5:5 – Suddenly the fingers of a human hand appeared and wrote on the plaster of the wall, near the lampstand in the royal palace. The king watched the hand as it wrote.

12. Prophetic Words

1 Timothy 1:18 – Timothy, my son, I am giving you this command in keeping with the prophecies once made about you, so that by recalling them you may fight the battle well,

13. Repetition

Jonah 3:1–2 – Then the word of the LORD came to Jonah a second time: "Go to the great city of Nineveh and proclaim to it the message I give you."

14. Remembering (Memory)

John 14:26 – But the Advocate, the Holy Spirit, whom the Father will send in my name, will teach you all things and will remind you of everything I have said to you.

15. Those in Authority (Spiritual Leaders)

Hebrews 13:17 – Have confidence in your leaders and submit to their authority, because they keep watch over you as those who must give an account. Do this so that their work will be a joy, not a burden, for that would be of no benefit to you.

16. The Ignorant (someone who doesn't know God's speaking through them)

John 11:49–52 – Then one of them, named Caiaphas, who was high priest that year, spoke up, "You know nothing at all! You do not realize that it is better for you that one man die for the people than that the whole nation perish." He did not say this on his own, but as high priest that year he prophesied that Jesus would die for the Jewish nation, and not only for that nation but also for the scattered children of God, to bring them together and make them one.

17. Strangers

Hebrews 13:2 – Do not forget to show hospitality to strangers, for by so doing some people have shown hospitality to angels without knowing it.

18. Angels

Acts 8:26 – Now an angel of the Lord said to Philip, "Go south to the road—the desert road—that goes down from Jerusalem to Gaza."

19. Trances (Out of body, you're in the vision)

Acts 10:10–13 – He became hungry and wanted something to eat, and while the meal was being prepared, he fell into a trance. He saw heaven opened and something like a large sheet being let down to earth by its four corners. It contained all kinds of four-footed animals, as well as reptiles and birds. Then a voice told him, "Get up, Peter. Kill and eat."

20. "Donkeys" (Strange and Unique ways)

Numbers 22:28 – Then the LORD opened the donkey's mouth, and it said to Balaam, "What have I done to you to make you beat me these three times?"

21. Fleeces (Confirmation)

Judges 6:36–40 – Gideon said to God, "If you will save Israel by my hand as you have promised—look, I will place a wool fleece on the threshing floor. If there is dew only on the fleece and all the ground is dry, then I will know that you will save Israel by my hand, as you said." And that is what happened. Gideon rose early the next day; he squeezed the fleece and wrung out the dew-- a bowlful of water. Then Gideon said to God, "Do not be angry with me. Let me make just one more request. Allow me one more test with the fleece, but this time make the fleece dry and let the ground be covered with dew." That night God did so. Only the fleece was dry; all the ground was covered with dew.

2 Corinthians 13:1 – This will be my third visit to you. "Every matter must be established by the testimony of two or three witnesses."

22. Peace
Colossians 3:15 – Let the peace of Christ rule in your hearts, since as members of one body you were called to peace. And be thankful.

2 Corinthians 2:12–13 – Now when I went to Troas to preach the gospel of Christ and found that the Lord had opened a door for me, I still had no peace of mind, because I did not find my brother Titus there. So I said goodbye to them and went on to Macedonia.

23. The Bible
2 Timothy 3:16–17 – All Scripture is God-breathed and is useful for teaching, rebuking, correcting and training in righteousness, so that the servant of God may be thoroughly equipped for every good work.

24. Living words from Scripture
Matthew 4:4 – Jesus answered, "It is written: 'Man shall not live on bread alone, but on every word that comes from the mouth of God.'"
Romans 10:17 – Consequently, faith comes from hearing the message, and the message is heard through the word about Christ.

Ephesians 6:17 – Take the helmet of salvation and the sword of the Spirit, which is the word of God.

25. "Coincidences" (God directed happenings)

Acts 1:26 – Then they cast lots, and the lot fell to Matthias; so he was added to the eleven apostles.

Proverbs 16:33 – The lot is cast into the lap, but its every decision is from the LORD.

26. Signs

Luke 2:12 – This will be a sign to you: You will find a baby wrapped in cloths and lying in a manger.

Isaiah 38:7 – This is the LORD's sign to you that the LORD will do what he has promised.

27. Prophetic Demonstration

Acts 21:11 – Coming over to us, he took Paul's belt, tied his own hands and feet with it and said, "The Holy Spirit says, 'In this way the Jewish leaders in Jerusalem will bind the owner of this belt and will hand him over to the Gentiles.'"

Healing Commands of Jesus

Be clean! (Matt 8:3)

Go! It will be done (Matt 8:13)

Go! your faith has made you well (Luke 17:19)

Little girl, I say to you, get up! (Mark 5:41)

Get up! (Luke 7:14)

Get up take your mat and go home! (John 5:8)

Come out! (John 11:43)

Stretch out your hand! (Matt 12:13)

I am willing (Luke 5:13)

Your faith has healed you (Matt 9:22, Mark 5:34)

Go, your faith has healed you (Mark 10:52)

Go in peace! (Luke 8:48)

Took them by the hand (Luke 8:54)

Take your mat and go home! (Mark 2:11)

Receive your sight (Luke 18:42)

Go away. The girl is not dead but asleep. They laughed he put them out. Took her by the hand (Matt 9:24-25)

Do you believe that I am able to do this? Touched their eyes - according to your faith (Matt 9:28-29)

Your request is granted (Matt 15:28)

You deaf and mute spirit, I command you, come out of him and never enter him again. (Mark 9:25)

What do you want me to do for you? Touched their eyes (Matt 20:32-33)

No more of this! (Luke 22:51)

www.ingramcontent.com/pod-product-compliance
Lightning Source LLC
Chambersburg PA
CBHW071317090426
42738CB00012B/2720

* 9 7 8 1 9 5 9 5 4 7 0 0 6 *